DIY COLOUR SERIES

HOME REPAIRS

AURA
EDITIONS

CONTENTS

Editor: Mary Lambert
Art editor: Gordon Robertson

Published by Aura Editions
2 Derby Road, Greenford, Middlesex

Produced by Marshall Cavendish Books Limited
58 Old Compton Street, London W1V 5PA

© Marshall Cavendish Limited 1985

ISBN 0 86307 278 X

Printed and bound in Hong Kong by Dai Nippon Printing Company

While every care has been taken to ensure that the information in *Home Repairs* is accurate,
individual circumstances may vary greatly. So proceed with caution,
especially where electrical, plumbing or structural work is involved.

CHAPTER 1

FLOORS AND WALLS

Loose, creaking floorboards, a cracked concrete floor, scuffed skirting and walls that offer no barrier against the elements—not entirely conducive to a healthy, sound home. But unless you're observant and thorough in your maintenance, threadbare carpets, draughts and stained wallcoverings could be the least of your troubles

FIXING FLOORBOARDS

Although solid and hardwearing, floorboard timbers are prone to all sorts of minor irritations and potentially structural faults. For instance, creaks under the carpet are annoying but not dangerous; rotten boards which collapse underfoot can be disastrous. Even if your floorboarding is in perfect condition, it may still need work to improve draughtproofing—or you may need to get to wiring or pipework underneath.

Types of floorboard

Most floorboards are made of softwood, usually pine. The boards are fixed at right-angles to the joists which support them, and may be nailed or screwed in place. The board ends are arranged to coincide with the joists, so that the join lies over the centre of the joist, for maximum support. Floorboards fall into two basic types: square-edged, and tongued-and-grooved (fig. H). Tongued-and-grooved (T&G) boards and their derivatives (see illustration) are

designed to eliminate draughty gaps but are more difficult to take up than their square-edged counterparts.

If you are in any doubt which of the two types is used for your flooring, choose two boards with a slight gap between them and slide a knife blade in as far as possible—compacted grime or draughtproofing in the gap may have to be scratched out first. If the blade is stopped, the boards are either tongued or rebated.

Lifting square-edged boards

For your starting point, choose the most convenient free end of the board you wish to lift. If the board extends right across the room and under the skirting on both sides, you have to start lifting it in the middle and

Below: *Use a strip of wood offcut to protect the surface of the floorboards when you are prising out tough, rusty old nails*

work gradually towards the ends. When all the nails are loose, you spring the board free by pulling it upwards into a bow shape.

To lift the board, insert a bolster into the joint gap between it and the board on one side, in line with the nails at the free end. Use a club hammer to drive it home. Then stamp on the bolster to push it down towards the floor (fig. B). Do the same on the other side of the board.

As the board is levered up, insert the claw of a hammer under the end and continue levering up from here until the board comes completely free of the joist.

For safety, immediately remove any exposed nails—particularly those left upright in the joists. A crowbar is much easier than a claw hammer for this job.

If a board proves particularly stubborn, try to free one end and insert a metal bar under it. Using the bar as a levering support, stamp on the free end. After each stamp there should be some 'give', so move the support along the board towards the next joist until the nails give way here.

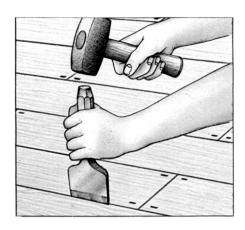

A. *A bolster is the ideal tool to break the tongues of T&G boards*

Lifting T&G board

Start by choosing a suitable free end and section of board, well clear of the skirting. To break the tongue, insert a bolster into the join between two adjacent boards at the end of the board you wish to lift (fig. A). Give the bolster a few sharp taps with a hammer, until you feel or hear the tongue below start to split. Continue until the split extends at least 75mm from the nails, or until you otherwise judge it to be clear of the joist. You can then replace the bolster with a saw, knowing that its blade will escape damage from floorboard nails.

You can use almost any type of saw but a compromise between the awkward length of a panel saw and the short length of usable blade on a tenon saw is a purpose-made *flooring saw* (fig. D).

If a power saw is used, set the sawing blade depth to about the thickness of the board to avoid any damage to the sub-floor (if any), or to pipes or wires suspended below the flooring.

B. *Loosening the edges of floorboards can also be easier with a bolster*

Continue cutting between the two boards until you are about 75mm from the next line of nails, and once again use the bolster to break the tongue along the stretch over the joists.

When the tongue is fully severed, use the bolster, claw hammer and metal bar to lever up the board as you would do to lift a square-edged one. In this case, though, concentrate your levering activities at the end and along the severed side of the board at each joist. You should be able to lift the nails and tilt the board enough for the interlocked side to slide free of the adjacent board.

Well-fitted tongued-and-grooved boards may be so tightly cramped together that splitting them apart with a bolster and hammer may not be possible without causing extensive damage to both boards. In this case, the board you wish to remove must be split lengthways at the middle. A power saw is the best type of tool for this job.

★ WATCH POINT ★

To help lift the rest of the board, insert a metal bar, length of stout timber or piping underneath the free end. Use the bolster and hammer to loosen the board at each line of nails, then lever it clear with the metal bar.

Cutting across floorboards

It is best to cut across a floorboard either over a joist or to the side of one, so that support for the new board ends is readily available. Cutting over a joist is a little more difficult than cutting beside one, but enables you to nail the cut section straight back in place.

Cutting on a joist: It is important to make the cut along the centre of the joist, otherwise one or other of the two freshly made board ends is not going to be supported properly.

The centre line of the joist can be pin-pointed by following on the line of nails of adjacent boards and board ends. Use a try square to pencil a cutting mark on a line joining the farthest possible reference points on each side of the board you are cutting. You can do this by eye or, better, by stretching a piece of string over the distance between the two points. If you are cutting alongside a board with a clearly indicated joist, just continue the line of the board end

C. *A claw hammer is a useful tool for lifting boards*

(or fixings) when marking the cutting line. If the nails are staggered, take a common centre line from as many boards as possible.

To make the cut, you can leave the board in place and use a padsaw or power jig saw. But if the board is long enough, it is easier to lift it up into a 'hump' and cut with a tenon saw or flooring saw. To do this, you lever the board upwards with the bolster and then support it with two offcuts of timber wedged beneath it.

Cutting beside a joist: First locate the side of the joist. You may be able to do this by inserting a knife or metal rule into the gap between the floorboards, sliding it along until it hits the joist. Mark the board at this point, and use a try square to complete the cutting line. Alternatively, and if there is a gap between the floorboards on the other side, repeat probing and simply join up the two points marked on the board (fig. 1).

Drill an 8mm hole up against and at one end of the cutting line (fig. 3) then use a padsaw or power jig saw to cut next to, and along, the cutting line. The padsaw can be replaced with a handsaw or circular-blade

D. *A flooring saw will easily cut out shorter lengths of board*

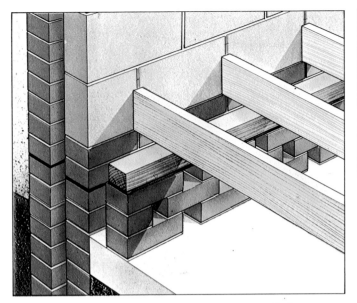

E. *Joists of a suspended floor are supported on small sleeper walls or piers on a concrete base*

F. *Metal joist hangers built into the inner wall are one method of supporting an upstairs floor*

G. *Flooring joists can also be built right into the inner section of two masonry walls*

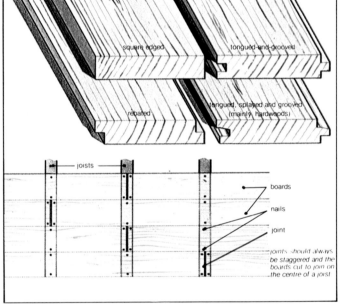

H. *Types of floorboard. Square-edged boards are found in older British houses, tongued boards elsewhere*

power saw when convenient, and re-used if necessary at the end of the cut.

Fitting an extra bearer

If you have removed a section of floorboard by cutting along the side of a joist, you must fit an extra timber bearer to the joist, in order to provide support for the new board end.

Make this bearer from an offcut of softwood, with minimum dimensions no less than 38mm by 50mm. Cut it to length, slightly longer than the width of floor-boarding removed and use either nails or screws for fixing it in place (fig. 9). If you choose nails, use two or three about 75mm long for each floorboard width, and hammer these partially into the broader side before positioning the bearer. If you use screws, two for each board width are enough, but drill pilot holes before fitting them.

Position the bearer against the joist and make sure that the top edges of both pieces of timber are exactly flush. Pull the bearer upwards, tightly against the floorboards on each side, while you hammer or screw it securely in place (fig. 10).

New square-edged boards

There are few problems in replacing square-edged boards. New ones of the same thickness are cut to length and—in the case of non-standard sizes—to width. If part of the board has to be tapered or otherwise shaped to fit, use the discarded board as an accurate

1 To remove a damaged section, first locate a joist position. Mark a cutting line either over the middle of the joist or to one side of it

2 Using a piece of wood as a guide, scratch and then tease a cut with the first few teeth if you are using a tenon saw to cut on the joist

3 If you are using a padsaw or power jig saw to make a cut beside a joist, drill a small hole the width of the blade

4 Use a padsaw or compass saw to cut right across the board or, if you prefer, just to give you a slot in which to start off your handsaw

5 A padsaw can be used to sever the tongue of a tongued-and-grooved board if other forms of sawing are impracticable

6 Remove nails from the joist using a claw hammer. Protect the board alongside with an offcut. Do not hammer old nails into the joists

7 When making an extra support, start by cutting a generous length of stout timber. The extra width ensures that the board is firmly fixed

8 Mark the floorboard gap on the upper surface of the bearer. As you can see, the bearer straddles the gap and acts just like the joist

9 Partly skew-nail the support, to the point when the nails are just about to break through on the other side of the timber

template when you saw to shape the replacement one.

If a single board is to be replaced simply slot it into place and nail down. A number of boards covering a large area are best fitted individually—if possible in the same flooring 'pattern' as originally. No two board ends should lie side by side on the same joist.

When fitting a number of boards, do a 'dry run' first to check the width fit, and whether tight butting of the boards is possible. Where the boards are to remain visible and not under carpeting, keep to the original spacings for the sake of the overall finished appearance.

If part of the original floorboarding is to be replaced, cut off any wood which is badly split where nails were removed. Do not re-use old nail holes. These, and new holes

along the complete length of the board, should be made good with a filler.

Replacing T&G boards

Replacing tongued-and-grooved boards is not quite so straightforward. If you are re-using the old board, this can be replaced by

fitting the remaining tongued or grooved side into the adjacent board. A small gap will remain on the other side—this must be carefully plugged for complete draught-proofing.

To fit a new tongued-and-grooved board, you may have to plane off its tongue to get it to fit, but you must leave its grooved side intact.

If a number of adjacent boards have been removed, any necessary combination of old and new boards may be used when reflooring. The technique is to loosely fit these together over the floor area to be covered, in the process forming a low arch by making the boards slightly over-sized. Lay a spare plank over this, and press or stamp the boards down: the tongues and grooves knit together in the process. The flattened boards can then be fixed in place.

10 *Complete the nailing while pushing the bearer against the joist and upwards against the fixed boards on both sides*

11 *If fitting a thicker board than the rest, a cut-out has to be made where the board crosses a joist. First mark the joist's position*

12 *Transfer the marks from the underside of the replacement floorboard to its edges. Repeat this step at every joist position*

16 *If the replacement board is too thin, use sheet wood to make up the difference. Do not use newspaper folds for this job*

17 *When replacing tongued boards the last two will need force before slipping into fit—use a mallet and protective wood offcut*

18 *Nailing boards into place. A pencil line ensures accuracy. A floor cramp—worth hiring for big jobs—keeps the boards tightly packed*

Alternatively, you can use a protective wood off-cut and mallet, as in fig. 17, to get them to fit.

Replacing short sections

If you are cutting out and replacing a short section of floorboard you may want to use up a spare piece of timber lying about the house. Alternatively, you may have difficulty getting a replacement board which exactly matches the thickness of your existing ones. Either way, the new board will be far better too thick than being too thin.

Having cut your new section to length, lay it beside the gap in the floor and mark off on the underside where it is to pass over a joist. Chisel out rough rebates between the marks, to the same depth as the board is oversize (fig. 14).

When you lay the board, the rebates should fit over the joists and allow it to rest flush with the others.

If the replacement board is too thin, nail a strip of hardboard (or other thin material) to the top of the joists to make up the difference.

Creaking boards

Loose and creaking floorboards may be caused by incorrect nailing, by the joists below them settling, or by warping and shrinkage. It is usually possible to cure a loose board simply by renailing or screwing it back in place. But before you do this, check that the loose joint coincides with the centre of the joist below, taking the board up if necessary. If it does not, widen the joist with a new bearer (figs. 7–10), or replace the whole board.

To nail floorboards, use 50mm lost-head nails or flooring nails. Position them next to, and about 12mm away from, the existing nails. When you have finished, drive all the nail heads well below the surface of the board with a nail punch to give a neat finish.

To secure floorboards with screws, use 40mm countersunk steel screws. Drill clearance holes for them 12mm from each existing nail, taking care that the holes go no deeper than the thickness of the board. When all the screws are in place, make sure that none of them protrudes above the surface by forming a recess with a countersink bit.

13 *Carefully cut the board in order not to exceed the required rebate depth—this can be gauged by sight or by direct measurement*

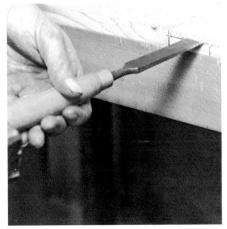

14 *Use a chisel to remove wood between the cutting lines. The chisel face should be down. Work in stages to end with a level cut*

15 *Check that the rebate fits snugly and is of the required depth. Continue chiselling if the board is proud of those alongside*

19 *If you decide to use nails for fixing a floorboard in place, hammer in the heads using a punch. Use filler and stain to conceal the hole*

20 *If you choose to screw down a board, drill a hole to accept the screw body only. This minimizes the effort needed in fixing boards*

21 *Use a countersink bit to drill a recess for the screw head and—if necessary—fill the hole once the board has been screwed to the joist*

SKIRTING TROUBLE

Skirting boards can be fixed to a wall in several ways. In timber-frame construction, they are simply nailed through the plasterboard and into the studs, or vertical timbers, behind.

In masonry walls, nails can be hammered at an angle through the board and its backing of plaster into the brickwork (fig. 22). Alternatively, strips of wood called grounds can be used. These are firmly attached to the wall and act as a fixing base for skirting boards placed over them. A continuous strip is supported at intervals by small upright pieces called soldiers (fig. B).

With either system, some plaster damage must be expected as the old skirtings are removed, and usually needs to be made good with plaster or filler before new boards are fixed.

In rare instances, the skirting is fixed to wedge-shaped uprights bedded into cavities in the brickwork (fig. C). Installed at the time the wall was made, these are held in place by a mortar filling which often decays over a period of time. Excessive force on the skirting—such as that required to remove it—is often sufficient to dislodge these uprights. If this happens, mortar them back in. A new upright can be made by tapering a suitable length of batten.

The golden rule to bear in mind when dealing with skirting board is to be careful; the bedding plaster is easily chipped by a casual knock.

Replacing boards

To remove a length of skirting, start at one of the corners and place a bolster on the top edge where the skirting meets the wall. Using a claw hammer, hammer the bolster gently down. This will prise the skirting away from the wall at that point. Continue this action along the length of skirting to be removed. Where greater resistance is met, the skirting is nailed to the wall.

With the top edge prised away from the wall you can start to remove the skirting completely. For this you need a claw hammer and a small, thin piece of plywood or hardboard to protect the wall finish. Place the claw of the hammer down behind the

Right: *Damaged skirting boards can be easily replaced with new boards. Several different methods can be used to fix the boards to the wall*

top edge of the board and slip the timber between the claw and the wall. Lever gently upwards on the handle, pressing the hammer head against the timber. This forces the board further away from the wall and draws out the nails at the same time.

Always use timber or a piece of hardboard to protect the wall or the hammer may leave an indent. Do not use a crowbar as this can damage the wall plaster.

Once the skirting is removed the nails should be pulled out. Use a pair of pincers to draw out the nails from the back of the

---

★ WATCH POINT ★

With the top edge of the board free, insert a timber wedge between the board and the wall at the place where the first cut is to be made. The wedge should have one sloping face and be thick enough to push the board out by about 40mm. Position the wedge with the flat face to the wall so that as you hammer it down, the sloping face pushes the skirting away from the wall.

---

board. This keeps the paint surface intact, as the face of the board often splinters if the nails are hammered through and drawn out from the front.

Partial removal of skirting

When the area of damaged or decayed skirting is relatively small, partial replacement is more economical. Measure the length of board to be replaced and buy or make a new piece to match. First, prise the damaged part of the board away from the wall with a bolster (fig. 1).

To cut out the damaged length of board, make a mitred cut at each end using a mitre block or box. There are no set rules for positioning the direction of the mitres: they can be parallel or they can face in opposite directions, and lean either inwards or outwards.

Position the mitre block with its back against the face of the skirting and the top level with, or above, the top of the skirting. If necessary, put some suitable packing material under the block to raise it to this level. Make the first cut at the end of the

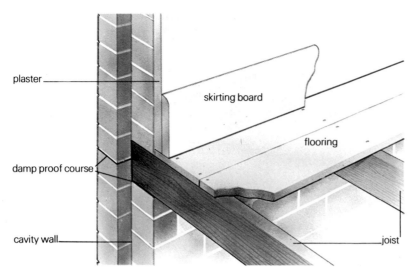

A. *Skirting fixed directly to a wall. On a plastered brick wall, plaster damage usually accompanies the skirting board's removal, especially if the nails securing the board have rusted*

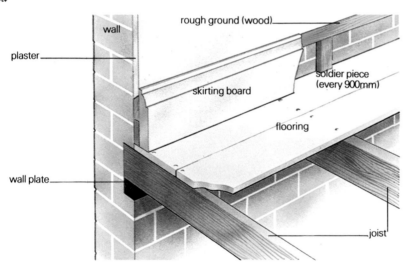

B. *Skirting fixed to a rough ground supported clear of the floor. Board removal may cause partial collapse of the ground and plaster base it supports*

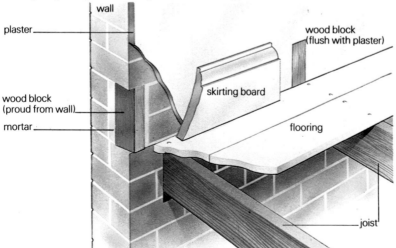

C. *Skirting fixed to wood blocks set in the wall at the time of building. Retaining mortar may have decayed, and both this and damp soldiers have to be made good before replacing skirting*

damaged area using a panel saw in short rapid strokes (fig. 6). Only the first few teeth of the saw are used so these teeth must be extremely sharp or they will just damage the wood.

Continue the rapid strokes until the teeth of the saw reach the base of the block. Remove the block in order to complete the cutting down to the floor, taking great care to maintain the straight line of the cut. Pull out the wedge and reposition it where the second cut is to be made at the other end of the damaged piece of skirting. The second cut is made in exactly the same way. Once free, lift out the damaged piece of board from the skirting.

Fitting the new board

Using the mitre block, cut a mitre at one end of the new board. Make sure that the direction of the cut is the same as that of the first cut, made when removing the damaged piece. After cutting the mitre, measure the inside edge of the area to be fitted with new skirting and transfer the measurement to the replacement board. Use the mitre block again to cut the second mitre. Check that the direction of the cut matches that in the skirting. Fit the replacement piece in the gap to check its compatibility. If adjustment is necessary, use a plane with the blade set finely and remove a few shavings from the end grain.

★ WATCH POINT ★

You can use masonry nails to fix the skirting into the brickwork behind. In this case, a piece of timber the same thickness as the plaster should be placed behind to overlap the old and new pieces of skirting at each end. This ensures that the skirting will not be pushed out of its vertical position should it be knocked at all from the bottom.

Fixing the new board

An easy method of fixing the new length of board is to use 38mm oval pins and skew nail them through the mitre joints. This way, you will nail through both thicknesses of skirting. Punch the nail heads below the surface, so that you will end up with a better finish, and then make good the indentations with a little woodworking filler.

1 *Place a bolster behind the top edge of the skirting board. Hammer the bolster down gently. Repeat along the length of skirting*

2 *Place the claw of the hammer behind the skirting and slip the protective board between it and the wall. Lever the board away*

3 *If a board proves particularly stubborn, hammer a row of wedges down behind it. This reduces the risk of splitting the board*

7 *You may have to match new board to old skirting. For a 'pencil round' mark a line 6mm from the front top edge and plane it round*

8 *For splayed skirting, mark the desired thickness on the top of the board and the end of the incline on the face. Then plane down*

9 *For splayed and rounded skirting, mark off the top of the board as for a pencil round and plane and sand the edge*

13 *Next, mark a mitre across the top of the board, joining this mark to the one on the back. Make sure the mitre slopes the right way*

14 *Cut through the board to form the mitre—either 'free-hand', as here, or using a mitre box or mitre block. A true cut is essential*

15 *Position the board to check for fit, remembering to remove bits of plaster or other obstructions. If necessary, trim it with the plane*

4 *When the whole length of skirting has been levered from the wall, draw out the nails from the board using a pair of pincers*

5 *If a damaged length is to be removed, first drive in a wedge, then place a mitre block against the skirting while you start your cut*

6 *Now continue the cut to the bottom of the board, having first ruled a vertical pencil line to help keep the cut straight*

10 *For an angled board, mark the correct thickness on the top of the board and the angle required on both the end grains. Plane down*

11 *A variety of skirting styles can be manufactured from ordinary board or from a combination of board and moulding*

12 *To join a new section part-way along a wall, first measure the length you need and mark it on the back of the replacement board*

16 *Another technique of fitting boards is to drill a well for the nail head and then fill this with filler after the nail has been hammered in*

17 *Nail the board into place once a fitting check has been made. Use suitable filler to conceal the nailwells you have drilled*

18 *The completed section should join inconspicuously with existing skirting if the job of matching and fitting has been properly done*

Matching new skirting to old

New houses usually have one of the following types of skirting: pencil round, splayed, splayed-and-rounded, or chamfered. These are easier to obtain than the elaborate older boards but fill-in pieces can be made from a square-edged board.

For pencil round skirting, for example, mark a line along the face of a square-edge board, about 6mm down from what will in effect be the top leading edge. Carefully round this edge as you plane down to the 6mm mark. It helps to start with the plane level, at the top, curving round the edge as you plane down the edge along its length.

Splayed skirting—where the face of the board is sloped slightly upwards—is almost as straightforward. Mark the desired thickness at the top, and where you want

---

★ WATCH POINT ★

You can make up many types of moulded skirting by gluing lengths of wood architrave (of which a good timber merchant should have a wide range) on top of a square-edged board. If this fails, ask a small joinery shop to make you new skirtings to match your old ones, using a short length of an old one as a pattern. But setting up the tooling is expensive, so this course is worthwhile only if you have several lengths to replace.

---

the face to end. Then plane down between these two lines.

Skirting a room

Skirting a whole room is in many ways much easier than repairing existing skirtings. You do not have the problem of matching new skirting to old and, as skirting can be purchased in full lengths to suit room walls, you will have no joints to make in the length of the boards.

The one rule when skirting a room is that external corners have a mitred joint and internal corners have a scribed one. Apart from that, it is sensible to work round the room in rotation. Doing this gives you a scribed cut at one end of a board. The other end will be either square cut (for another scribed joint) or mitred, depending on whether the board meets another internal or external corner.

When using masonry nails always wear plastic goggles as the nails are brittle and are inclined to break off if they meet resistance in the brickwork.

External corners

Mitred joints pose no problem if made carefully with a cutting guide such as a mitre block. However, once placed against the wall, the inevitable irregularities in the plaster may cause a few small gaps to develop. Fill these with filler paste: when they are dry and have been decorated they will not show.

If you can, make these mitred cuts with a mitre box and panel saw. If not, use a jig saw with an adjustable sole plate. First, mark a piece of board to length and cut it 50mm oversize. Hold it in place against the wall

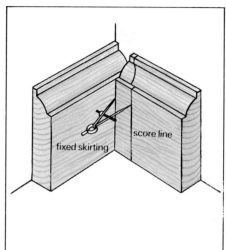

D. *Dividers can be very useful to scribe complex shapes of moulding to a new board*

19 *For an external corner, hold the board against the wall and mark in pencil the end of the wall with a straightedge*

20 *Add to this the thickness of the board. Draw a line across the face. Set the jig saw blade to the width of the sole plate*

23 *Cut a mitre on a second length of board. Measure off and cut to length, leaving a square end to go into the inside corner*

24 *Using a keyhole saw, cut along the outline on the face of the board which has been displayed by cutting the mitre first*

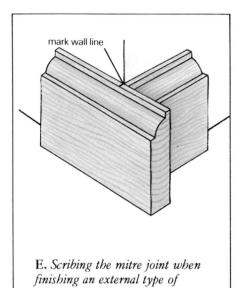

E. *Scribing the mitre joint when finishing an external type of corner*

and carefully mark the inner measurement of the mitre joint. To do this, hold a straightedge or try square at right-angles to the board and close against the other wall. Add the width of the board to this measurement and mark off in pencil, continuing the line all the way down the face of the board.

Set the sole plate on the jig saw to an angle of 45 degrees (instructions for this accompany the different makes of saw). Cramp the board firmly—face upwards—and set the jig saw blade against the pencil line. Mark on the board the right-hand edge of the jig saw sole plate and extend this line across the board. Measure the gap between the lines at both ends to check that the line is straight.

Take a small timber offcut and cramp it firmly in place against the line. This provides a straight and secure edge against

which to press the sole plate. Saw across the board keeping the plate pressed closely against the offcut and the result will be a perfectly cut mitre.

Cut a second mitre on the adjoining length of board, using the jig saw in exactly the same way.

Now position the first length of board against the wall and measure right from the tip of the mitre to the wall to determine the exact length you will need. Transfer this measurement to the board and then cut a square edge for the butt joint with a panel saw.

Before nailing the skirting to the wall, a replacement ground must be fitted if the old one is no longer intact or has rotted. Use masonry nails to fix the grounds into the brickwork, below the plaster (see fig. B). Mark the position of the soldiers on the floorboard below, so that you know where to nail when the skirting board has covered them. Use nails to fix the skirting to the ground support and punch the heads below the surface so that they can be concealed with filler.

Internal corners

A scribed joint is used on internal angles. You cut one board to length with a square end, then cut the second to a shape that fits against the curved or moulded end of the first board. This joint is used because, unlike a mitre, it cannot open up—leaving a gap between the boards—as you nail the skirtings to the walls.

There are two ways of obtaining the scribed shape on the second board. One is to use a pair of dividers to trace the profile of one board onto the other. Then cut out this profile with a coping saw, keyhole saw or jig saw.

A better way is to start by fixing the first board (the square-ended one) in place. Then, on the second board, cut a mitre. This leaves a profiled outline on the surface of the board. So cramp the board firmly and cut around this outline—at right-angles to the board's surface—with your coping saw, keyhole saw or jig saw.

However you fix the skirting to the wall or ground, make sure the board is firmly in place—particularly where knocks are common, such as near doorways, sockets and external corners that are always in an exposed position. A firm fixing can prevent considerable additional damage to plaster and grounds that ought really to have been replaced a long time before they even worked loose.

21 *Cramp an offcut to this mark and set the saw blade to 45°. Saw along the pencil line, pressing the sole plate firmly against the offcut*

22 *Fix this board to the wall with masonry nails. Take care when hammering to avoid brickwork or plaster damage beneath*

25 *Join the two boards with two or three nails, nailing through one mitred edge into the other. Punch the nail heads down*

26 *Measure and cut the board to length to fit over the square end of the previous length of board. To get a perfect fit, tap it down*

DEFENCES AGAINST DAMP

Brick is a porous material and moisture can penetrate it. If the brick walls of a house are properly built, then damp should not be able to get through to the inside surfaces. But if the walls are defective, then damp can strike.

The tell-tale signs are damp, discoloured patches frequently accompanied by a white salty deposit called efflorescence and perhaps a fungal growth. However, condensation has much the same symptoms—so you should check first that this is not the cause.

Unfortunately, when penetrating damp becomes visible it is already too late to prevent some damage to the plaster and wallcoverings. But prompt action will keep this to a minimum.

Tracing the source

Damp can penetrate the exterior fabric of a house in all kinds of places. If you discover that a DPC is at fault or that a roof covering is leaking badly, wholesale replacement of the defective material may be the only answer. But most penetrating damp problems are due to smaller defects and can be cured a great deal more easily.

External cures

These vary, according to the nature and location of the damage.

Around chimney stacks: Older types of chimney stacks, particularly those which are exposed to the elements, provide a common place for damp to enter and work its way down the internal walls. Flue gases condensing inside the stack cause the mortar joints to expand, and this, combined

Below: *Damp patches should be left to dry out and then sealed before redecorating*

with wind and rain, results in rapid deterioration of the brickwork. Damp can also penetrate the flashings around the roof if these have been neglected or badly installed.

If, after investigation, you discover that the mortar joints are at fault, it is worth repointing the entire stack using a 1:3 mortar mix with waterproofing agent added.

If the flashings are suspect, cut them out and replace them completely. Apply waterproof mastic at all the joints.

Parapet walls: Very badly pointed or damaged parapet walls give rise to similar damp problems. They should be carefully checked and thoroughly cleaned before broken bricks are made good. Repoint using the 1:3 mix with waterproofer added.

In some older houses, the parapets were not fitted with a DPC. In this case, you may have no choice but to remove the copings and first few courses, then insert your own

1 *A transparent silicone-based water-proofer can be applied to outside walls to prevent damp seeping through bricks and mortar*

2 *Flaking plaster and fungal growth on walls should be thoroughly cleared by the vigorous use of a wire brush all over the area*

3 *Mark around the outside of the affected area so that all of the unsound plaster can be chopped out with a hammer and wide bolster*

4 *Cut out all the affected plaster until the brickwork underneath is exposed. This can be cleaned down and left to dry out*

5 *Before and during the period of drying out—which may take a few weeks—a fungicide should be applied to the whole area*

6 *Once all signs of damp have disappeared, coat the brickwork with bitumastic paint before filling the gap with sound plaster*

DPC of bituminous felt.

Another common fault is that rainwater runs off the top of the copings, down underneath them, and so on into the brickwork below. To stop this, you must cut a 'drip' groove along the underside of the coping stones on the side which faces the roof, 25mm from the edge. Do this either with an electric angle grinder or with a small bolster and club hammer. Be sure to wear safety goggles to protect your eyes from flying masonry.

Sometimes, cutting an accurate groove in this way is impossible. In this case a less satisfactory solution is to secure a 15mm square batten to the underside of the stones. Make sure that the wood is well soaked in preservative, then secure it with an epoxy resin adhesive. Do not use screws or

---

★ WATCH POINT ★

When you are searching outside, do not assume that the entry point of the damp is directly adjacent to the damp patches on the internal walls. Damp can often enter well away from the point where it eventually manifests itself, so a thorough inspection of the external walls and their junction with the roof is essential.

---

masonry pins as these will split the wood and allow damp to penetrate it. Remember, though, that this is only a short-lived cure and shouldn't be treated as a lasting repair.

Gutters and downpipes: If you find after periods of heavy rain that damp patches appear adjacent to a gutter or downpipe, start by making a thorough check of your rainwater system and remove blockages.

Ogee-section guttering—which is screwed directly to the fascia boards—often splits along the back vertical face and is a particularly common source of damp. So, too, are old cast-iron and galvanized steel downpipes: these may look to be sound but a closer inspection often reveals that the backs have rotted away. Long, rust-stained water marks down the brickwork are often the most obvious signs of rot in the guttering.

The only satisfactory solution to these problems is to renew the offending section.

Rendering: If your house is rendered, damp may still have penetrated even though the surface appears to be sound. Constant expansion and contraction due to weathering can cause the render to detach itself from the brickwork and craze.

Check whether this is the case by tapping the rendering in several places with a hammer handle—a hollow sound will reveal where it is loose. When the render is 'blown' in this way, you must cut it back to sound edges and fill the hole with new render.

Bridged DPC: A very common cause of penetrating damp, especially around floor level, is that the DPC has been covered or bridged outside the house. Soil or debris may be piled high above DPC level if you have been gardening or building near outside walls, so allowing damp to find its way into the brickwork. Timber and other objects stacked against the outside walls are another possible source of dampness: they too should be removed.

Remove any such material immediately and make sure that a gap of at least 150mm is left between the DPC and ground level.

Dirty wall ties: Random patches of damp which appear after heavy rain may be an indication that debris such as brick-laying mortar has collected on the metal ties between the inner and outer leaf of a cavity wall, causing damp to penetrate along them. This is typically the result of careless building or repair work carried out on the walls.

The only remedy is to cut away the brickwork around each patch, identify the offending tie, clean it and make good. This can be a laborious process: you may be able to save time by cutting only the bricks around a central patch, then poking a stick along the cavity to clean the other ties.

7 *The small gaps around doors and window frames which allow damp to enter must be stopped by forcing mastic between the joints*

8 *Once the mastic has been applied, the surface can be smoothed down with a small piece of rounded stick periodically doused in water*

12 *Seal the wall with a primer and then cut the laminate to length, allowing extra at the top and bottom for trimming*

13 *Brush water evenly and liberally on to the back of the laminate so that it becomes thoroughly saturated and tacky to the touch*

Repairing brickwork

One of the most common causes of penetrating damp is brickwork which has been allowed to deteriorate. In this case the damp can appear suddenly and cause damage over a wide area.

In less serious cases, the pointing breaks down and falls out and the bricks become badly pitted due to weathering. In the worst cases, in very cold conditions, the bricks become *spalled*—water enters the cracks, freezes, then forces the faces off.

If bad pointing is the problem, repoint the wall and cut out and replace any bricks which are badly damaged. Powdery mortar and brickwork should be sealed with PVA bonding solution after you have raked out the joints.

★ WATCH POINT ★

If you want to keep the existing brick finish, an alternative to the conventional exterior paints is transparent, silicone-based waterproofer. This protects the brickwork but does nothing to detract from its appearance. And though it prevents damp entering the wall, it allows the moisture already there to escape freely.

When using this type of waterproofer, take extra care with your initial surface preparation as it is this which affects the quality of the final finish.

Where the state of the brickwork is generally poor but still intact, consider applying a cement- or stone-based paint. This can often improve the appearance of the house and, providing it is regularly maintained, is effective at keeping out damp.

Before you apply the paint you must thoroughly prepare the surface, first by running over it with a wire brush to remove loose debris, then by painting on a fungicide to kill any mould growth which still remains. Repoint any areas of loose mortar and apply bonding solution to suspect areas.

Doors and windows

Another site of penetrating damp is around door and window frames, where gaps have

9 *Use a hammer and bolster to cut a drip groove along the underside of a masonry window sill so that it runs in a line 25mm from the edge*

10 *As an alternative, a 15mm square batten of wood soaked in preservative can be secured under the sill with an epoxy resin adhesive*

11 *Before applying a damp barrier, rub down all damp patches to remove flaking paint and allow the wall to dry out thoroughly*

14 *Fold the laminate over on itself towards the middle with the wet side inwards and leave it in this state for one hour*

15 *Once primer has dried, paint the adhesive evenly and thinly on to the wall, covering an area wide enough for one length of laminate*

16 *Apply the wet side of the laminate to the wall, brushing it into place and starting from the top. Subsequent rolls should overlap by 12mm*

appeared due to shrinkage or weathering. Putting mastic in the gaps can cure this.

Start from the top of the frame, working the point of the applicator right into the gaps and making sure that they are well filled (fig. 7). Then use a small piece of dowel, which has been wetted, to force the mastic deep into any smaller cracks and wipe away the excess (fig. 8).

A less obvious cause of damp around windows is that the drip groove beneath the sill is blocked or damaged, causing water to run along the underside of the sill and into the brickwork. Make sure that it is cleared, cut a new one with hammer and chisel, or, for a temporary cure only, fit a 15mm square wood batten under the sill, about 25mm from the edge. The batten must first be coated with preservative, then secured with an epoxy adhesive (figs 9 and 10).

★ WATCH POINT ★

Remember that drying out walls will take some time—often a number of weeks—so do not get impatient or try to speed the process by using heating in the room; this is likely to give a false impression of how successful you have been with your external cures.

Internal cures

It is wrong to believe that you can cure penetrating damp internally: you must first stop it at source by working on the external walls as has already been described. Though

temporary repairs are sometimes possible, any work you do on the inside should be regarded as an addition to the work you have done outside, rather than as a final cure.

Always avoid the temptation to cover up areas of dampness which appear internally with paint or wallcoverings—the damp will only reappear later.

The general practice is to carry out remedial work outside the house and then allow the inside to dry out thoroughly. Give this as much encouragement as possible by opening windows and doors; if you have carried out the work properly, you should see the patches of damp recede.

Once you are convinced that the wall has dried out, you must remove all the wallcoverings and cut away any patches of damp or blown plaster with a hammer and bolster. If only sections of the wall are affected, the bare brickwork should be cleaned and painted with bitumastic paint, then covered with sound plaster. But if the damage is more extensive, it is best to dry line the whole wall or alternatively cover the affected area with a protective damp-proof barrier.

Applying a damp barrier: If areas of damp persist on internal walls, you can apply a damp barrier. This comes in kit form and consists of a waterproof laminate which is stuck directly to the affected wall, once the surface has been prepared with a special primer. Though not as complete a treatment as dry lining, it has the added advantage that you do not have to go to the trouble of removing all the old plaster before you install it.

First prepare the walls by removing old existing wallpaper, making good any blown or damp plaster and smoothing down high spots with glasspaper (fig. 11). You should also remove the skirting board since the damp barrier must be carried down behind it.

After sealing the wall with primer, the laminate can be hung in strips much as you would with wallpaper (see figs 11 to 16).

Dry lining the wall: This involves covering the bare brickwork with a pitch-impregnated fibre sheet to shut out the last traces of damp and protect new decoration. The sheet, which is corrugated, comes in rolls 1m wide by 5m long (fig. A).

Having stripped off all the affected plaster, fix the sheets to the bare brickwork with galvanized clout or masonry nails. Firmly drive the nails through the corrugated valleys at spaced intervals of about 300mm.

Where the sheets join, line the wall behind them with 100mm wide pieces of bituminized felt laid vertically to stop the damp getting through, then overlap the sheets by one corrugation. Where the lining material is cut to fit around pipes or other wall fixtures, fill the gaps with a waterproof mastic.

When you are lining only one wall, stop the damp getting round the edges of the sheets by continuing the lining some way around the corners of the adjacent walls. For the same reason, you should try also to carry the lining 150mm below floorboard level. At the junction with the ceiling, leave about a 150mm gap to allow air to freely circulate—this can be easily covered later with coving.

Once the lining is in position, you can either replaster the wall or else fit sheets of foil-backed plasterboard.

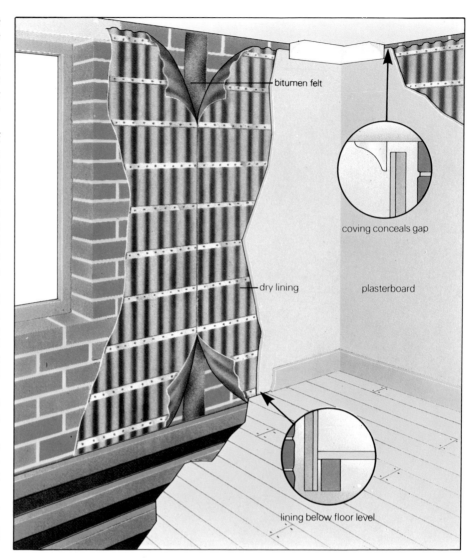

A. To dryline a wall, you will need to cut away all the damp plaster and cover the exposed brickwork with pitch-impregnated sheeting

Basement walls often suffer from damp. The cure may be a simple matter of patching up with waterproofing compound, repairing pipes, clearing out drains, or taking steps to cure condensation. If the basement has been damp for a long time and the damp is quite extensive but cannot be traced to a single source or location, then you have a reasonably major job on your hands.

In the long term, in many cases, the only way to cure severe dampness in a basement is to 'tank' it. This involves waterproofing the entire basement—walls and floor—with a continuous membrane. You treat the basement literally as a tank—except it keeps water out rather than in.

The waterproof membrane can be several layers of a bituminous coating, with extra coats of bituminous paint, or rolls of bitumen impregnated felt fixed with a hot bitumen adhesive. In both cases particular attention has to be paid to joints and corners, and you'll have to take great care not to puncture the covering when attaching fixtures afterwards.

An alternative is to use a proprietary waterproofer. However, it is essential to plaster the walls and lay a floor screed afterwards.

Another approach is to fix pitch impregnated fibre material to the walls.

Before installing this, the floor slab has to have a waterproof membrane which is run up the wall for 100mm or so.

In very serious cases, the pressure of ground water may be enough to force off any waterproofing. If this happens, you will have to build a second wall in brick or concrete—what is in effect a box—within the basement with the water barrier actually sandwiched in between the two main walls.

HANDRAIL REPAIRS

The balustrade—the handrail and baluster assembly—is the most vulnerable element of any staircase to damage. But repairs are possible and should be made quickly for the sake of safety as much as appearance.

Securing loose balusters

If an individual baluster works loose the problem usually lies in its fixing and can be remedied.

Skew-nailed balusters (fig. A) are the most frequently and easily damaged—a blow can dislodge the butt joint and loosen the nails that secure them.

To secure the baluster properly you first need to remove it. Mark its position on the handrail and stringer, then tap the top end 'upstairs' and the bottom end 'downstairs'. Protect the baluster with an offcut as you hammer. Repeat until you can actually remove the baluster or—better still—the nails that hold it in place.

As an aid to repositioning the baluster in line with the others later, place a straightedge across the two adjacent balusters and draw lines on the handrail and stringer to intersect with your previous marks.

Remove the nails and clean the ends of the baluster and the areas to which it attaches. Test fit the baluster against your marks and use a spirit level to check that it will be vertical.

Clamp an offcut of wood to the handrail on the *downstairs* side of the baluster (fig. 1)—it will support the baluster in place as you secure it. Remove the baluster and clamp it in a vice or portable workbench.

Use a 4.5mm bit to drill through the holes already made by the nails, then countersink each hole. Slip a variety of No. 8 screws into the holes until you find ones long enough to project from the ends by at least 12mm.

Apply PVA woodworking adhesive to the ends of the baluster before screwing it in

---

★ WATCH POINT ★

If the baluster is to fit under a sloping handrail, use the broken baluster as a template to mark the angle at which the new one must be cut—check your marks against an existing baluster.

---

place—first to the handrail then to the stringer—with 38mm or 32mm screws.

Jointed types of baluster (fig. C) can sometimes work loose because of damage to the baluster, joint, handrail or stringer.

Inspect the ends for signs of damage. If the lower end is held by a housing joint (fig. D) it may be that the nosing on the stringer that completes the joint is loose. Renailing and gluing the nosing should be sufficient.

If the stringer or handrail is damaged around the joint, cut out the damaged section and replace it with a patch of new wood trimmed to size. Glue and pin the patch over the baluster, then plane and sand smooth the new area.

If the joint is simply loose, cut slivers of wood to fit the gap, apply adhesive and tap home firmly. Trim off the excess with a chisel.

Damaged balusters

Modern balusters are often square-sectioned battens and finding matching timber is no problem. However, in old houses they are frequently ornately turned spindles which can prove difficult and expensive to renew—especially if they aren't a standard pattern. Consequently it's often worthwhile trying to repair a broken one.

To remove the broken baluster, start by finding out how it is held in place. If it is mortised into a socket at one end only, you will be able to prise it out from the unmortised end. If it is mortised at the top but housed behind a nosing at the bottom, prise off the nosing and lever out the bottom end first. Where the baluster is mortised at both ends, saw through the bottom end flush with the stair or stringer, chisel out the old tenon and replace it with a wood plug.

Once you've got the baluster free, check the break. If the baluster has broken fairly cleanly at its thinnest point, try applying PVA adhesive to both surfaces and clamping them together until the glue has dried. If there isn't sufficient contact between the parts, drill into both ends and insert a glued dowel to strengthen the joint.

Where the wood has split at an angle,

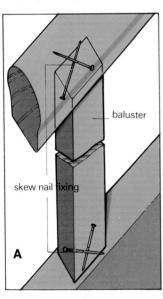

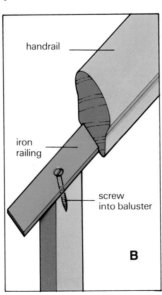

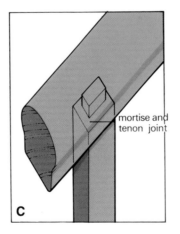

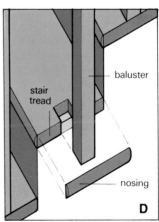

Above and left: **A.** *A skew-nailed baluster.* **B.** *A baluster screwed to steel rail.* **C.** *Mortise and tenon fixing.* **D.** *A housing joint in an open stringer*

1 *To remove a nailed baluster, you need to knock the top end 'upstairs'*

2 *Mark the exact position of the baluster under the rail with a pen or pencil*

3 *Clamp a support to the rail before you finally secure the baluster*

4 *If the break is clean and easily fits together, try gluing the pieces together*

there will be a larger contact area and you can screw and glue it together. Apply adhesive to both surfaces and clamp them together. Drill one or two holes—depending on space—at an angle through the thickest part of the break. Countersink the holes, then insert screws: drive the heads beneath the surface of the wood and cover them with matching wood stopping.

With the repair completed, apply adhesive to the ends of the baluster and slot it into place. Skew nail the baluster in position on the stringer with 40mm or 50mm lost head oval nails or by drilling and screwing as previously described.

Renewing a baluster

Renewing balusters calls for a slightly different procedure. If you need to replace the jointed type of baluster with a new one, start by measuring the height from the underside of the handrail into the recess in the step or stringer. Bear in mind that unless you can prise off the nosing you will not be able to slip the new baluster into the housings at both ends.

In this case, you must patch the mortise hole in the stringer with a wooden plug and skew nail the baluster directly to the patch after you have glued it into its housing at the handrail end.

Hold the replacement against one of the secure balusters, align the pattern and mark the position of the handrail and stringer on to the replacement. Cut to size using these marks as an accurate guide—add the housing depth.

Place the bottom end of the new baluster into its recess and tap the top end gently into position under the handrail. Mark for an angled screw fixing, then clamp an offcut of wood to the handrail so that the baluster rests against it. Completely remove the baluster so that you can drill an angled 4.5mm countersunk hole.

E. Fit a new section of stair handrail using a screw which is purpose-made

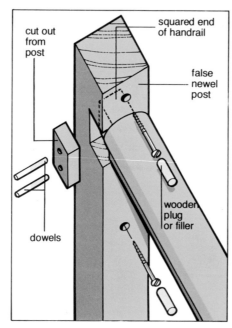

F. A housing joint is the neatest, easiest way of fixing a handrail to a false newel

Finally, you should replace the baluster and screw it to the handrail using No. 8 woodscrews—don't use nails.

Handrail repairs

Where just a section of handrail is badly damaged, it's worth trying to cut it out and renew it—replacing an entire handrail is expensive.

Start by carefully removing the balusters on each side of the damage. Saw through the handrail at a 45° angle at both ends of the damaged section.

If the top of the rail is fairly flat, you might be able to do this with a jig saw with the sole plate set to the correct angle but it's more likely that you will have to cut through by hand and tailor the new section to fit your cuts, whatever the angle.

Some handrails have a separate cap that sits on top of the handrail for the full run. Remove the cap by unplugging and releasing its fixing screws and prising it off before you saw through the handrail. Measure how much new handrail you'll need and take a section of the old handrail to buy an exact match.

Mark the ends of the new section to match the gap you've made direct from one to the other. Remember to leave a small allowance at each end before you saw and trim to fit. To join the new piece to the existing handrail, you will need a special fitting at each end—a handrail screw or bolt.

The former have a screw at one end and a bolt at the other while the latter have a bolt at both ends (fig. 6). The bolt end is secured by a special slotted nut which can be tightened with a screwdriver. You'll also have to insert 6mm dowels at each side of the handrail screw—the screws will pull the new section and the handrail together, while the dowels will prevent the new part twisting.

Lining up the holes for the handrail screws and dowels is simple if you use marker pins. Tap a 30mm panel pin about 20mm into one of the cut ends of the new

5 *For a stronger join, you will need to insert a thoroughly glued dowel*

6 *An angled break can be joined again using some countersunk screws*

7 *Use the broken baluster as a template to accurately mark the angle of the handrail*

8 *An extra bracket will strengthen a wall handrail more than adequately*

section of handrail exactly where you want the screws and dowels to be. Use a pair of pincers to snip off the ends of the pins a few millimetres above the surface. Repeat the same procedure at the other end of the section.

Place the new section of handrail in position. Push the existing handrail hard against the new section and then remove it. The cut ends of the pins should have marked the drilling position for the new handrail screw and the dowels. Remove the pins with a pair of pincers or pliers, then use a drill bit the same diameter as the bolt ends of the handrail screws to drill holes in the ends of the existing handrail.

You'll also need to drill 6mm dowel holes in the ends of the existing rail and the new section. Next, drill holes underneath the existing handrail to meet the bolt holes and make slots large enough to take the nuts which secure the handrail section. The holes should be positioned at a distance from the edge which is approximately equal to one quarter of the length of bolt section of the screw.

Coat the dowels with PVA adhesive, then place them into the holes already drilled in the replacement section.

With the slotted nuts in position, jiggle the new section into position. You'll have to spring open the gap in the rail and fit one end and then the other. Use a screwdriver to tighten up the slotted nuts.

Distorted handrails that have separated from the balusters need special attention. Take up the gap with a lath pinned and glued to the underside of the handrail and refit the balusters.

Damaged newel post

Newel posts rarely sustain damage, but if they do you must replace the whole post with a matching new one. They're available in a wide range of shapes and sizes.

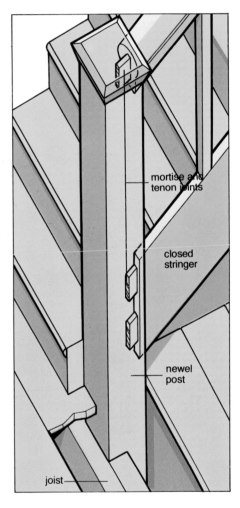

G. *Most newel posts are actually bolted to a joist situated under the floor. The stringer and the handrail are then firmly secured together with straightforward mortise and tenon joints*

If the floor is wooden, newel posts are generally bolted to a floor joist (fig. G). If the floor is solid, they're generally sunk in the concrete. The handrail and stringer is joined to the same newel posts with mortise and tenon joints that are strengthened with pegs drilled through the tenons (fig. G).

Remove the posts in sections—drill out the pegs then prise the joints apart. Use the old newel post and the handrail and stringer to reproduce the joints as the replacement post.

Refix the newel post in the manner used for the old one—assemble the mortise and tenon joints first then complete the base fixture. Soak the base in preservative for at least 24 hours.

Strengthen the fixing by adding a false newel post and fixing it to the wall with screws and wallplugs at 200mm intervals (fig. F).

It's easiest if you use the false newel post to mark the handrail end, then cut the handrail—by saw and chisel—so that it has a square end as shown. Then you can make a cut-out in the newel to accept the easier shape of the handrail. Fix the newel to the wall with screws and wallplugs, then attach the cut-out with woodworking adhesive and dowels.

Wall handrails

Separate wall-mounted handrails may be fixed by one of two methods: brackets mounted on the underside, or by screws and plugs. Strengthen bracketed handrails either by adding new steel mounting brackets between the existing ones or by removing one bracket at a time, re-positioning them and drilling fresh holes in the wall. Use sturdy screws—at least 50mm No. 10 gauge.

Directly fixed handrails may be strengthened by adding extra screws—the length of the screws will depend on the width of the handrail. First drill 6mm countersunk holes through the lower portion of the rail and then insert a smaller diameter masonry bit—No. 8 gauge—to drill the wall beneath. Make sure the holes are at right-angles. Use plastic strip wall-plugs cut to length to support the screws.

CHAPTER 2

ELECTRICS

Mending a blown fuse isn't complicated; and it's something all householders should know how to tackle with confidence. But if that fuse should repeatedly blow, this could be a signal that there's a far more serious problem afoot. Finding your way safely through the maze of cables that constitute your home's lighting and power circuits demands meticulous care and a thorough knowledge of how the system works

FIXING FAULTY FUSES

A circuit fuse is relatively simple to mend, but when a fuse continues to blow each time you replace it, either the circuit is overloaded—in which case you should switch off some appliances—or there is a serious fault somewhere along it which must be located and rectified before the circuit will function again. On no account must you replace the blown fuse with a length of wire or any other bridge, such as a nail. To do so would be tantamount to lighting a fire.

Having a thorough understanding of the theory of fuses and the faults which cause them to blow will help you to maintain the electrical circuits around the home. And even if you do not intend to carry out the repair work yourself, being able to locate the area of a fault will help to save on the cost of repair.

Why fuses blow

A fuse is a deliberately weak link included in the wiring of a circuit. If a surge of current occurs in the circuit, caused by a wiring fault of some kind or by overloading, the thin fuse wire is melted by the resulting extra heat generated by the current surge.

Fuses often blow because two wires in the circuit are in contact with one another. If the live and neutral wires make contact, this is called a short circuit; when the live wire touches the earth it is called a line/earth fault or a short to earth. Or the live wire may be in contact with earthed metalwork—such as the box of a flush-mounted light switch—to which the earthing core is attached via the earth terminal.

Although a fuse is a 'weak' link in the wiring, it requires quite a large amount of current before it blows. For example, a cartridge fuse requires a current of one and a half times its current rating before it melts, and a wire fuse may take a current of twice its rating. This means that under certain conditions, a 5 amp wire fuse may take a current surge of up to 9 amps for some time before it blows.

But when a short circuit occurs, the resulting current surge is enormous. This is also the case with a line/earth fault—if the earthing is in good condition. If the earthing is faulty, there may be insufficient current to blow the fuse in which case the fault will remain undetected and a potential fire hazard—the earth return will heat up due to the high resistance it meets.

Above: *When more than one appliance or light stops working, your first move should be to inspect each of the main fuses. Before touching the fuse box make sure that the main switch is turned off*

Checking the plug fuse

If an appliance goes dead but none of the others fed from sockets on the same circuit seem to be affected, suspect a blown plug fuse. If you have not already done so, switch off before opening up the plug. The fuse may look charred or it may not—but in any case you must check the appliance, the flex and the plug for faults before fitting a new one.

First of all check the rating of the fuse —and then the wattage of the appliance. If the former is only 3 amps and the latter is over 750 watts, you've found the fault. Follow on by looking at the plug connections: they should all be tight and there should be no stray strands that could short from one to another.

Check the plug in the socket. If it's a loose fit, one or the other may be badly worn and in need of replacement. Move on to the flex. It should be tightly held in the plug's cord grip. Along its length, there should be no evidence of fraying, splitting,

kinking or twisting—any of which may cause a blown fuse.

Finally, check the appliance. Start with where the flex enters it—the rubber grommet should be intact and there should be no appreciable movement when you pull it. If there is, this indicates loose terminals or cord grips inside.

Often, misuse or maltreatment of an appliance can blow a fuse. For example, an excessive build-up of dust or dirt can cause overheating, and the same problem results from restricting the airflow around it—particularly on hi-fi systems and videos. Foreign objects, too, cause problems and bear in mind that something may have fallen in accidentally.

If, after checking, you replace the fuse and it blows again, lose no time in having the appliance checked by an electrician.

Damaged flexes can be replaced in part (using an extension box) or in their entirety, but make certain that you take a sample of the old one with you to the shop so that the rating of the replacement can be matched exactly.

A fault in an electrical appliance is unlikely to keep blowing the circuit fuse, if the circuit is protected by a cartridge fuse in the appliance's plug. But a circuit fuse may blow if the circuit is heavily overloaded —drawing far too much current.

Overloaded circuits

Overloading is perhaps the most common cause of blown fuses. When an electrical wire is asked to carry more current than it can handle it heats up. Hopefully, as they are designed this way, the wire that heats up fastest is the fuse.

It is a common fallacy to suppose that just because a 15 amp power circuit can supply several sockets, so a single socket should, via an adaptor, be able to supply two or even three appliances. Often, the socket connections, adaptor and plugs simply cannot handle all that is asked of them. They heat up, the insulation begins to break down and the circuit fuse blows.

Electric cable and flex sizes are carefully determined not only by the amount of electrical current they can handle but also by how far they can carry it. Consequently, overlong flexes and extension leads or circuits which extend further than the guidelines laid down by the IEE (Institute of Electrical Engineers) can result in current surges which blow fuses—sometimes after years of trouble-free service.

Miniature circuit breakers

All the faults and checks described below apply equally whether your consumer unit is fitted with wire or cartridge fuses, or with miniature circuit breakers. A miniature circuit breaker (MCB) is a single-pole switch which is automatically cut off when excessive current caused by a fault flows through the circuit.

The principal differences between MCBs and normal fuses are that they require less current to shut them off than is needed to blow a fuse of the same current rating, and they operate more quickly. When a fault in the circuit persists, the circuit breaker trips immediately an attempt is made to switch it on. However, it is advisable not to switch on the MCB more than twice under fault conditions or you may blow the overload unit.

Cable faults

If a circuit fuse continues to blow each time it is replaced, a possible cause is that two wires are in contact with each other somewhere along the cable of the circuit.

If the wiring in your home is old, persistent fuse blowing may just be an indication that the wiring needs replacing

1 *In the case of a blowing fuse in a lighting circuit, replace the fuse then test each light. Start your checks at the lampholder*

2 *Next check that the wires in the ceiling rose are intact and that there is no contact between a naked earth wire and a live terminal*

4 *A typical source of trouble is an unsheated earth wire coming into contact with a live terminal behind the switch plate*

5 *The best way to insulate the bare insulation wire is to disconnect it, then slip on a length of green and yellow PVC*

altogether. For instance, older houses may still be wired with rubber-insulated cable which has a life of only about 25 years. After this time it may begin to break up, causing short circuits all along the wiring.

Make some initial checks on the cable. Turn off the electricity and open up sockets, light switches and ceiling roses all over the house. Make sure that the cable used in each case is of the correct type and rating.

If you find any old, rubber sheathed cable, your house must be rewired immediately. Some houses still have old round-pin sockets working off an obsolete radial circuit. These are dangerous—the circuits must be disconnected at the fuse board. Over-long circuits are a problem in houses wired on the radial system—the symptoms are usually that of circuit overloading. Suspect it if the circuit seems to extend

round the whole house; treat the circuit with respect until it can be rewired.

Faulty junction boxes found on light circuits using this method of wiring may need attention. Lift upstairs floorboards and look in the roof space for signs of deterioration or poor connections at boxes.

Trying to locate a specific fault on a relatively recent cable is a tedious job, which is best left to an expert using special test equipment, especially where the cables run under floors and are recessed into the walls. But it is still worthwhile knowing the possible cause of cable failure if only to narrow down the area of investigation.

Cables are often damaged in the course of alterations to a home, so begin by checking the wiring around the site of any recent work. For instance, if you have been fixing floorboards a nail may have penetrated a

3 *If necessary—and possible—inspect the underfloor junction boxes for clues such as smokey discoloration or melted insulation*

6 *In the case of slight damage to the neutral or live wires, bind the affected portion tightly with insulating tape and then refit the switch*

cable causing a short circuit or line/earth fault. And cables which are chased into masonry walls without a proper conduit are sometimes damaged by nails or screws.

Also check any recently installed wiring: you may have disturbed the old when running additional cable to new lights or socket outlets, or you may have failed to make proper connections to the new wiring.

If there is no reason to believe that the cable has been damaged when working on the house, you can investigate other, more accessible parts of the specific circuit as described below.

Lighting circuits

If the main fuse of a lighting circuit (one supplying only lighting outlets) keeps blowing, turn off all the light switches fed by that circuit, shut off the electricity supply at the mains then replace the fuse.

Turn on the main switch, then switch on each light switch in turn. When the fuse blows, you will have found the part of the circuit in which the fault lies. Now you must track it down.

The first thing to check is the flexible wiring which connects the lampholder to the ceiling rose. This may be worn or damaged, particularly if it is of the obsolete, twisted twin type. Once more, turn off the electricity supply and remove the relevant fuse holder. At the light, unscrew the lampholder to check the condition of the flex and make sure that the cores are securely connected to the terminals. If necessary, renew the faulty flex.

Now check the wiring in the ceiling rose by unscrewing the cover from the base which is fixed to the ceiling. A common problem here is that the earth wires are left unsheathed and make contact with one of the live terminals in the rose. If you find that this is the case, disconnect the wires from the earthing terminal, slip lengths of green and yellow PVC sleeving over them—leaving about 6mm of bare wire protruding—then reconnect them to the terminal.

Where a bare earth wire is not the problem, check the condition of the remaining wires. If the insulation of these is all intact and they are connected tightly to the correct terminals, replace the rose cover and turn your attention to the light switch itself.

Remove the cover plate of the switch and check the wiring. The most likely fault is, again, that the earth wire is bare and in contact with the live terminal. But it may be that the fixing screws of the cover plate have penetrated the insulation of one of the wires and that, with a flush-mounted switch, a section of live wire is in contact with the earthed metal box.

If it is the live return wire that is damaged in this way, the fuse will blow only when the switch is turned on; but if it is the live feed wire which is damaged, the fuse will blow whether it is on or off. The latter fault is easily recognized by the burnt insulation and smoke marks around the damaged area.

Where the area of damage is slight, you can make do by firmly wrapping some insulating tape around the bare section then laying the wires carefully back into the box so that the screws will not interfere with them. But if the damage is particularly bad—such as where a wire has almost been severed—the relevant length of cable must be replaced.

If, after examining the lampholder, ceiling rose, switch and any accessible cable you are still unable to find the fault, call in expert help. On no account be tempted to make a temporary 'repair' by fitting a fuse of a higher amp rating.

Power circuits

When the circuit fuse of a ring mains circuit continues to blow, the fault is unlikely to be in one of the portable appliances plugged into the circuit: when these are faulty, the cartridge fuse in the plug will blow leaving the circuit fuse intact. However, before you start work on locating the fault, unplug all appliances and check that the fuse in each plug is of the correct amp rating. Also switch off any fixed appliances at their fused connection units.

On a ring mains, the next step is to check the 30 amp main fuse. Very occasionally, when the circuit is already loaded to near its capacity, a fault on a small appliance may cause it to blow.

Other than an overload or a damaged circuit cable, the most likely fault in a ring mains circuit is in the mounting box behind one of the socket outlets. Switch off the electricity supply at the mains and examine each socket in turn.

Unscrew the cover plate of the first socket and examine the wiring attached to the terminals on the back: the likely faults are similar to those found in lighting switches.

Earth wires are often left uninsulated and therefore can easily make contact with the live terminal. This is particularly likely on a socket outlet as the earthing core is connected to a terminal on the back of the socket plate, rather than to one on the box, and can therefore be bent into a dangerous position as the plate is fixed.

Sleeve any bare earth wires in lengths of green and yellow PVC sleeving, then check the insulation of the live and neutral wires. These sometimes perish if the terminals are not tightened properly or where a cheap—or faulty—plug or adaptor has been used in the socket and has overheated. Alternatively, the insulation may have been pierced by the socket's fixing screws. Deal with this problem as described above and, if necessary, use shorter screws to fix the socket plate into place.

When you have checked the first socket, replace the cover plate and move on to the next. Even if you think you have found and rectified the fault, it is worthwhile checking the remaining socket outlets: if the fault was

7 *In the case of a ring mains circuit it is necessary to check each socket in turn. A common fault is a bared earth touching a live wire*

caused by a bare earth wire, it is likely that the other earth wires are unsleeved. And in any case, it is safer to risk blowing a 5 amp fuse than one of 30 amps.

If you do not find anything wrong with any of the sockets, the fault probably lies somewhere along the cable of the circuit, so it is best to call in expert assistance.

Immersion heaters

An immersion heater is usually supplied directly from its own circuit fuse with no other fuse intervening. When this circuit fuse blows, the fault is most likely to be in the immersion heater itself and therefore requires expert attention.

When the heater is supplied from the ring circuit—nowadays considered bad practice—it is connected either by a fused plug and a socket outlet, or to a fused spur outlet. So a fault which occurs in the heater itself should blow the local fuse, not the main circuit fuse.

8 *First disconnect the unsheathed earth wire and refit the loose live wire to the live terminal in the socket housing*

★ WATCH POINT ★

Tracing faults on other sorts of circuit follows much the same methods as described above. First switch off at the mains, then unplug or disconnect all appliances and switch off lights on the faulty circuit. Switch on the mains, and carefully re-connect all appliances and switch on lights one by one until you find what causes the fuse to blow. Then check them all out.

Mending a fuse

The first rule of mending a fuse is turn off the electricity—at the socket if it's a plug fuse, at the main switch if it's a circuit fuse.

The second rule is find out what caused the fuse to blow and to put it right.

The third rule is never use fuses or fuse wire of an incorrect rating—no matter for

9 *Then sheath the earth wire with a length of green and yellow PVC sleeving and secure it to the socket before refitting the assembly*

how short a time.

Plug fuse: Simply open up the plug, flick out the old fuse with a screwdriver and slot the new one in. In the case of fused connection units, the fuseholder either unscrews or is prised out with a screwdriver. Slot in the new fuse and replace.

Circuit fuse (cartridge): Remove the fuseholder of the circuit that has failed. Dig out the old fuse and slot in its replacement.

Circuit fuse (rewirable): These may be one of several patterns, notably open or enclosed, but the principles are the same.

Remove the fuseholder and loosen the screw terminals to release any burnt wire.

Cut off sufficient new wire of the correct rating to stretch the length of the holder and wrap around the terminals.

Wrap one end clockwise round one of the terminals and tighten. Feed the wire across or through the holder as necessary.

Wrap this end round the other terminal and tighten. Replace the fuseholder.

MCBs and ELCBs: Simply press the reset button once the fault has been put right.

10 *Ensure that the fuse wire you use is of the correct rating for that fuse*

11 *You must also make sure you use the correct rating of cartridge fuse*

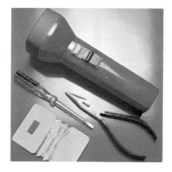

12 *Keep some tools close to the consumer unit to make repairs easier*

13 *Only reset a circuit breaker after locating and correcting the fault*

CHAPTER 3

DOORS AND WINDOWS

Doors and windows need regular attention to keep them in efficient working order. Minor repairs are quite straightforward and if a door needs to be re-hung, you'll find this no problem if you follow a few basic rules. A window, too, can be cured of typical problems—sticking and broken sash cords. And if a pane of glass should be smashed, replacement can be undertaken with ease

DOOR REPAIRS

There is nothing more annoying than a door which is difficult to open and close. And although the trouble can usually be put right quite easily, neglecting such a door may cause more extensive damage which is costly and difficult to repair at a later date.

Before attempting any repairs, it is worth considering what hinges are available and how you hang a door properly. Indeed, when a door hangs badly, the hinges are often at fault: either they are fitted badly or the wrong ones have been used.

Choosing hinges

Plastic, nylon, or—better still—pressed steel hinges are suitable for light internal doors, but if you are fitting hinges to a heavy outside door, use the strong type made of cast steel. If you want a finish which is rust free, jam free and decorative, brass hinges look good but are more expensive and less durable.

By finding out the thickness, weight and height of your door, you can estimate what size of hinge you require. For example, a lightweight door, 32mm thick, would need a 75mm × 25mm hinge whereas a heavier door, 45mm thick, might require a 100mm × 38mm hinge. Be careful not to buy a hinge which is too wide for the door as this will result in a weak, narrow strip of wood where the hinge is fitted. To find the size of a hinge, first measure its length, then the width of one of its leaves to the middle of the knuckle where it swivels.

Most doors are fitted with butt hinges and you can buy either the fixed or the rising variety. The rising butt hinge allows the door to rise as it is opened but shut down closely on to a carpet or threshold as it closes. This means that though the door does not scrape against floor coverings, it will stop draughts and reduce fire hazards once it is shut.

Rising butt hinges are either right- or left-handed, so decide which way you want your door to open before you buy a set. Avoid confusion by getting the difference clear in your own mind.

Marking and fitting

Before you fit the hinge decide which side you want the door to open. Panelled doors

Above: *This kitchen is cramped by a door which opens inwards. By rehanging it to open outwards more space is created*

can be hinged on either edge but most modern flush doors can only be fitted with hinges on one edge.

On some doors the hinge positions are marked on the edge of the door and these areas are usually reinforced, so it is advisable not to try to fix hinges to any other spots.

Once you have decided which edge of the door is to be hinged, arrange it so that it is resting on the opposite edge. Support the door by wedging it into a corner, cramping it to the leg of a table, or by holding it in a vice (fig. 1).

The best positions for the hinges are 215mm from the top of the door and 225mm from the bottom, but make sure that this does not leave them over any joints or the door may be weakened.

Use a marking knife and try square to mark the hinge positions on the door edge, starting from the knuckle edge where the hinge will swivel. Mark across all but 6mm of the edge then continue on to the face of the door, marking the thickness of one hinge leaf (fig. 2).

Next, open one of the hinges and lay it in position on the door edge to check that the lines you have drawn are accurate. Hold the hinge in position and use a marking knife to mark each end (fig. 3). Then scribe the width and depth of a hinge leaf on to the door edge and frame (figs 4 and 5).

Cutting out

The hinge recesses are now ready to be cut out. Use a bevel-edged chisel and start by chopping downwards across the grain in a series of cuts 5–6mm apart (fig. 6). Leave a thin uncut border of about 2–3mm around the three edges (fig. 6). Now hold the chisel flat, bevel side up and pare away the

1 *Before fixing hinges, stand the door on edge and support it securely with a vice firmly clamped to one end of the door*

2 *Position the hinges 215mm from the top of the door and 225mm from the base, keeping them well clear of any joints*

3 *Use a marking knife and try square to mark the hinge position on the door edge. Here, the leaf thickness is marked on the face*

4 *Then set a marking gauge to the width of a hinge leaf and scribe this on the door edge between the two lines previously marked*

5 *Reset your marking gauge to the depth of one hinge leaf and mark this on to the face of the door frame between the two knife cuts*

6 *Use a bevel-edged chisel to cut out the hinge recesses. Make a number of cuts 5–6mm apart, to leave an uncut border around the edge*

chipped-up timber. Finally, keep the flat side of the chisel parallel to the door edge and clean out the rest of the recess (fig. 7).

The hinge should now press firmly into place flush with the surrounding timber. You may have trouble with some types of hinges which are bent slightly due to pressure in their manufacture. If this is the case, pare away a further 1–2mm from the recess.

Fixing hinges

Once the hinge is comfortably in position, carefully mark the screw holes with a sharp

A. Right: *Holes left in the frame by relocating the lock, keyhole and handle need to be filled with wood*

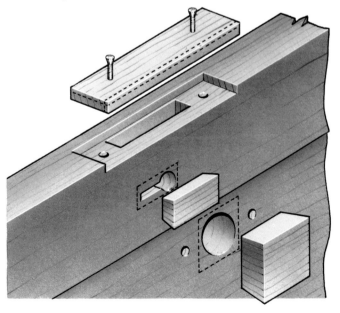

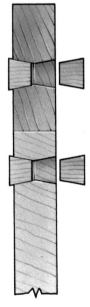

7 *Cut out the chipped-out timber in the hinge recesses with a chisel—held bevel side up—until the recess is clean and smooth*

8 *Mark the screw holes slightly off centre towards the inside of the recesses. This allows the hinge to bed securely once it is fixed*

9 *Once you have drilled pilot and clearance holes, insert the screws so that they are slightly below the level of the hinge plates*

pencil then remove the hinge and re-mark the screw centres with a centre punch. Try to mark these a little off centre—towards inside of the recess—so that once the screws are inserted, the hinge will be pulled snugly into position (fig. 8).

Drill pilot holes to the depth of the screws and then clearance holes deep enough for the screw shanks. For heavy butt hinges use 38mm No. 7 or No. 8 screws. Insert the screws so that they finish level with, or slightly below, the hinge plate (fig. 9).

If you are using brass screws, put in a steel screw first. This will cut a thread in the wood and avoid the possibility of shearing off or damaging the soft brass screw heads.

Fitting the door

Position the door in its frame by supporting the base with wooden wedges made from offcuts (fig. 10). Both door and hinges should be in the fully open position unless you are using rising butt hinges, in which case they should be closed.

With all types of hinge, make an allowance at the base of the door for any proposed floor covering and adjust the gap as necessary by altering the positions of the wedges. When you are satisfied that the door is in the right place, scribe around the hinges with a marking knife to mark their positions on the door frame.

With the door removed from the frame, mark out the hinge recesses—their length,

B. Right: *Badly weakened areas need to be replaced with dowelled sections. Cut along line A-A, then B-A*

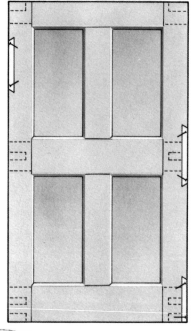

12 *The holes can be filled with glued 15mm thick dowels, chamfered at one end and with longitudinal saw cuts*

width and depth—accurately with a marking knife and adjustable try square. Use the same technique to cut the recesses as you used for those on the door.

Replace the door and position it exactly using the wooden wedges, then tap the hinge leaves into place in the waiting recesses. Finally, mark and pre-drill each screw hole then insert one screw in each hinge so that you can check that the door opens and closes properly. If it sticks at any point, make minor adjustments by chiselling away more of the rebates before you drive home the remaining screws.

Sticking doors

If a door sticks and you can find nothing

10 *Wooden wedges made from offcuts can be placed under the foot of the door so that it can be positioned to fit the frame exactly*

11 *Broken or damaged joints can be strengthened by first drilling out the old wedges to a depth of 75mm using a 15mm twist drill*

13 *When removing a planted door stop, first use a blunt, wide chisel and a mallet to prise the stop away from the door frame*

14 *By inserting the claws of a hammer into the gap, the door stop can then be worked loose and away from the frame*

wrong with the hinges, it may be that part of the door frame has swollen. Where the swelling is slight and there is plenty of clearance between door and frame, investigate the possibility of bringing the swollen part away from the frame by either packing or deepening one of the hinge recesses. Be sure to make only the slightest adjustments in one go, or the door may stick elsewhere around the frame.

Where the swelling is more severe, you have no choice but to plane off the excess and redecorate the door. The planing can be done with the door *in situ* providing you first wedge the base to take the weight off the hinges.

Older doors and those particularly exposed to damp may warp or become loose at the joints, causing them to fit badly in

their frames. In the case of slight warping, one answer is to make a small adjustment to one of the hinge positions so that you take up the twist. Do this on the frame—not on the door.

However, a more satisfactory solution is to remove the door so that you can cramp and strengthen the frame. Take off all the door furniture—the hinges, knob, lock, key escutcheon—place it flat on a workbench, then cramp the frame square using a sash cramp with a long bar.

Where gaps appear in the joints, scrape out any dust, accumulated grime and old glue with a chisel or knife. Then bring the joints together by cramping across the frame in two or more places. Use softwood offcuts to protect the door from being bruised by the cramps.

Next, drill out the old wedges holding the tenons at each frame joint to a depth of 75mm (fig. 11); use a 15mm twist drill bit. Make up some 85mm lengths of 15mm dowel with longitudinal cuts in them to allow for compressing (fig. 12) and chamfers at one end to give a snug fit.

Liberally smear each piece of dowel with external grade waterproof woodworking adhesive then drive them home into the drill holes with a mallet. Check that the cramps are still holding the frame square by measuring across the diagonals—which should be equal—and leave the adhesive to set. When it is dry, cut off the excess dowel with a tenon saw and finish the edges in the normal way.

Repairing a stile or rail

If a stile or rail is split, it is usually possible to open this up, force in some adhesive then cramp it closed again. In this case, where necessary, place some newspaper between the split and the cramp protective offcuts to stop the latter from sticking to the frame. When the adhesive has set, fill any remaining cracks with wood filler and finish with a block and glasspaper.

Very badly damaged or rotten areas must be cut out completely and replaced with new timber. Using an adjustable bevel and marking gauge, determine and mark out the extent of the damage along the frame. Mark the width of the damaged area with a marking gauge on the face of the door.

You must now cut out the timber. In the example shown in fig. B, you would make

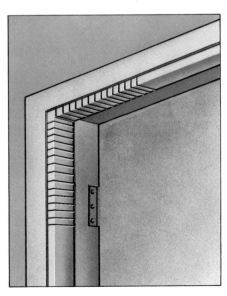

C. Left: *Remove a rebated door stop by first making a series of cuts around the corners of the frame*

15 *To remove a rebated stop, make a series of cuts around the corners. Chop out the waste and cut away the remainder of the stop*

16 *When rehanging a door which was hinged on the other side pin pieces of wood block to fill the gaps and plane smooth*

17 *If the door is rehinged to swing in a different direction, a new door stop must be added so that the door will close properly*

the internal cuts A-A by drilling through the wood then finishing with a padsaw or powered jig saw. Make the cuts B-A with a tenon saw, remove the damaged section, and smooth the cut edges with a wide, bevel-edged chisel.

Mark out and cut a replacement section, making it slightly wider than the frame so that it can be planed flush after fixing. Secure the section with woodworking adhesive and oval nails, the latter punched well below the surface level.

If the replacement section is over a joint, the tenon in that joint will have been seriously weakened by the repair. The remedy is to drive two or three dowels through the new timber into what is left of the tenon (fig. B). Drill and glue the dowels as described above.

★ WATCH POINT ★

If you decide to change the side on which the door hangs, all the operations detailed will be necessary and you will have to swop over the door furniture to the other side.

Make good the holes left in the door by driving in tapered and glued wood blocks. When you have done this, fill any remaining gaps with wood filler and repaint the door.

The stop is bound to be securely fixed and you may have to use considerable force. The job becomes easier when you can insert the claws of a claw hammer and ease the

stop away, working upwards from the base of the door (fig. 14).

Once the door stop has given way, remove any old glue or chipped wood with a chisel, plane and glasspaper.

Removing a rebated stop: Start by measuring by how much the stop protrudes then mark this amount down and around the outside face of the frame with a marking gauge.

Next, take a tenon saw and make a series of cuts 12–18mm apart in the top corners of the door frame (fig. C). Remove the waste between these with a wide chisel. This done, you can insert a rip saw or power saw and cut downwards through the remainder of the door stop. Afterwards, plane the cut timber flush with the rest of the frame and use a chisel to clean up the corners (fig. 15).

Changing direction

It is often useful to change the direction in which a door swings—to make more space in a small room for example—or to hang it from the opposite side of the frame.

Making a door open in the opposite direction involves removing and resiting the door stop, altering the hinge rebates and possibly changing the door furniture. You may or may not have to change the hinges, depending on what type you have. Ordinary butt hinges can simply be used the other way up.

How you go about the job depends on whether your door stop is simply planted —nailed to the frame—or rebated into it.
Removing a planted stop: Remove the door from the frame and clear the space around you. Then use a blunt, wide chisel and mallet to cut into the joint between stop and frame and lever the latter away (fig. 13).

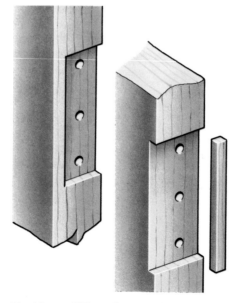

D. Above: *When changing the direction of opening, the hinge recess has to be moved to the opposite edge*

Rehanging

When you come to rehang the door, the hinge recesses may well have to be moved. Do this by chiselling them across to the other side of the frame. Then make up wood blocks to fill the now unused parts of the recesses and pin and glue these in place (fig. 16).

Refit the door stops—or make up new planted ones in the case of rebated stops—in accordance with the new door position. Make sure that the stops are firmly pinned and glued (fig. 17).

If the door lock or latch is handed, you must exchange it for a new one and fit it according to the manufacturer's instructions. Alter the position of the striker plate and make good the old recess as you did the hinge recesses. Finally, rehang the door as described above; start by fitting the hinges.

REPLACING BROKEN GLASS

Above: *It is sensible to replace the glass of a broken ground-floor window as soon as possible to deter any would-be intruders*

Apart from the danger of exposed broken glass, a smashed window in the home is an open invitation to an intruder. You can reduce both risks by reglazing the window yourself. The job requires care but is straightforward and quick.

If you are reglazing a downstairs window it should not be necessary to remove the window from its frame. But if the window is upstairs, you need an extension ladder to reach the outside of the window. In this case, the job will take longer and you may find it more convenient to take the window out of its frame and reglaze it on a workbench at ground level.

A hinged sash can be removed from its window frame by unscrewing the hinges. Use a bradawl to scrape out paint from the screw heads. To remove a sash from a double-hung window means removing woodwork, so in the case of an upstairs window, it may be better to work from a ladder.

If you decide to work from the ladder, secure it at the top by looping a thick rope through the rungs and tying it to a screw-eye fixed in the wall. Additionally, make sure the feet of the ladder are well anchored with a sandbag, or tied to stakes driven into the ground. Rest the feet on a board if the ground is soft.

A useful tip is to wear an apron or workman's overall which has large tool pockets so that you can carry everything likely to be needed for the job. This will save countless trips up and down the ladder during the course of the installation.

Removing broken glass

Take particular care when you are removing broken glass from its frame. Always wear thick (leather) gloves to pull out loose pieces (fig. 1).

Stubborn slivers must be smashed out with a hammer. But before you do this, cover both sides of the glass with thick cloth or blanket to prevent chips flying. For additional safety, wear goggles or old sunglasses at all times.

If you have removed the window from the main frame, cover it and lay it on several sheets of newspaper before you knock out the glass. This will make it easier to gather up the splinters afterwards.

After you have hammered out the glass, carefully remove the covering cloth and work loose fragments left in the frame. You should be able to prise out the glass quite easily, but if the putty is very old and hard and the glass refuses to be teased loose, cover the window with a cloth again and smash the fragments down to the level of the putty. Then, wearing eye protection, use a hammer and chisel to knock out the remaining putty with the glass embedded in it.

The old putty can be removed with a *hacking knife*—a tool specifically designed for this job—but a chisel will do the job nearly as well. Make sure that the chisel is an old one, well past its useful life, as it will become quite blunt when used in this way. Remove all the putty, including the bedding layer, and take care not to damage the wood with whatever tools you use (fig. 2). Where hacking off the old putty has exposed areas of bare wood, prime these and let them dry before you apply putty over them.

Measuring up the pane

When measuring up for the new pane of glass, always take the measurements twice: a mistake of only a few millimetres can make the pane unusable. Also, measure each opening within the main frame separately as small size differences between any two can go unnoticed until it comes to reglazing.

When giving measurements to the glass merchant, it is customary to give the height before the width. This way, if you are buying frosted or patterned glass, the pattern will be the correct way up (vertical)

A. Below: *Cross-section showing the normal method of glazing with putty. Triangular-shaped nails, called sprigs, are used to hold the pane in place against the back putty. These are then covered by more putty*

when you install it. Check this with the supplier when you buy.

The glass

Glass is now graded by thickness in millimetres—it was formerly graded by weight per square foot—and for most applications 4mm is adequate, although 3mm is sufficient for smaller windows. *Float glass* is now the most commonly used for general purpose work but cheaper *horticultural glass* may be used where viewing distortion is no problem—such as in a greenhouse.

★ WATCH POINT ★

When you have determined the final height and width measurements of the window, subtract about 3mm from each to allow sufficient clearance in the frame—subtract 6mm in the case of slightly warped frames.

For help and advice on the choice and safe use of glass, do not be afraid to consult your local glass supplier. Several types of glass can be used around the house and it is important to use a strengthened form where there is risk of breakage. For example, UK recommendations state that only toughened or laminated glass should be used for balustrades which protect a difference in floor levels or which are used for shower

B. Below: *Wooden beading can be used in place of the set of sprigs. This results in a neater-looking finished job which many prefer to the more common putty glazing method where greater skill is required*

screens.

Wired and laminated glass can both be used for floor-level windows, and those near to stairs (such as in a hall) can also benefit from these types.

A wide variety of decorative glass is available in addition to standard frosted patterns; using these in place of clear glass for extra privacy is well worth considering.

Before you install the glass, place and check it for fit in the frame and, if necessary, get the supplier to make small adjustments. You can sometimes accommodate very small irregularities by turning the sheet upside down or around in relation to the frame and then trying it again.

1 *Carefully work loose the large fragments of glass, then tap out the smaller pieces. Wear heavy-duty gloves when handling the glass*

5 *Push the replacement pane into position but apply pressure at the edges only. The bedding putty seal should be even and unbroken*

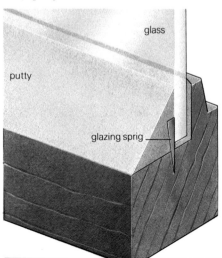

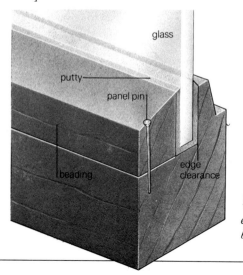

Using putty

Putty needs to be of the right consistency if it is to hold the glass in place and form a watertight seal. And when first taken from the tin it is inclined to be too wet, rather sticky and consequently difficult to handle. Knead it gently between the palms of your hands or place it between folds of newspaper to remove excess moisture and oil.

There are two types of putty: linseed oil putty for wooden-framed windows, and metal casement putty for use with metal frames. The latter should also be used as a bedding seal if metal-framed glass—such as insulating glass—is fixed into a wooden frame. In this case, linseed oil putty is used to finish off the outside seal.

Installing the glass

Once you have checked the glass for fit, lay a strip of bedding putty around the window frame (fig. 4). Use the heel of your hand to smear the nodules of putty around the insides of the rebates.

Place the glass in the frame and push it gently but firmly against the bedding putty. Push around the outside of the frame—not the middle—with a pad of cloth to protect you against any slivers of old glass left in the frame. As you do this, the putty will ooze out on the other side.

The bedding putty is necessary not only for providing a good watertight seal, but because it also takes up small irregularities in the trueness of the rebate. A final depth of up to about 5mm is recommended, and you can ensure an even depth around the frame by locating small wooden spacers such as spent matches.

The sheet of glass must be centred within the frame—you should already have had it cut to measurements slightly smaller than the frame's inner dimensions. The best way of doing this is to stick matchsticks between

2 *Use an old chisel or a hacking knife to remove hardened putty. Be especially careful of slivers of glass that may be embedded in this*

3 *Take particular care to clean out the upper rebate in a vertical sash window, but beware of glass slivers stuck in old putty here*

4 *Apply small nodules to the frame rebate so that sufficient back putty depth results. Use the heel of your hand to force putty home*

6 *Use a hammer or old chisel to tap the glazing sprigs home and slide the head along the glass to avoid cracking the pane*

7 *Trim off the bedding putty by a straight cut with the putty knife. Then apply the facing putty and smooth this down to finish*

8 *When the putty has matured, four weeks or so afterwards, it must be painted over to prevent it from drying out completely*

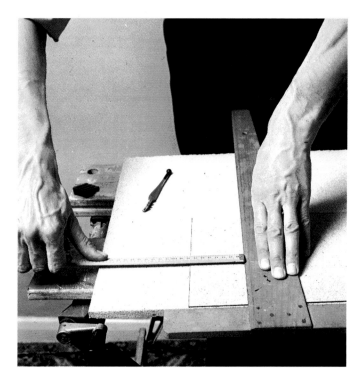

C. *Lay the glass on a cleaned and perfectly level work surface, such as a sheet of chipboard. Measure off the cutting line accurately, positioning a wooden set square or other suitable straightedge at the mark. Do not use a wax pencil for marking as this may affect the efficiency of the cutter*

D. *Score a line by running the cutter along the straightedge in a single continuous stroke. A score line is made on one side only. You can lubricate the cutter and the cutting line with white spirit (turpentine) beforehand, but this is considered necessary only for thicker glass. Cut decorative glass on the smooth side*

E. *Place the straightedge beneath the glass and tap firmly along the score line to 'spread' the cut. This stage is particularly important as it reduces the risk of an incomplete break along the score line, which can be difficult to rectify afterwards. To concentrate the effect of the score line, run the cutter only once*

F. *Arrange the glass sheet so the cutting line coincides with the straightedge, place a sheet of newspaper or card over the glass sheet and push the 'waste' end sharply and firmly downwards to break the sheet along the score line. Small tail pieces can be nibbled away carefully, using pliers or the indentations on the cutter*

the glass edge and frame at odd points around the window; or use folds of thin wood or card to build up greater depths. Spacers should not be necessary if you can work on the window flat.

When the sheet of glass is properly bedded, by which time it should remain in position by itself, secure the glass on each side of the frame by tapping home a couple of *glazing sprigs* (fig. 6) with a pin hammer or an old chisel. Sprigs are small, headless nails, buried by the face putty when the glazing is completed. On larger windows, use more sprigs at 150mm spacings around the frame. Start with the bottom edge and then deal with the top and side edges.

When this is done, you can apply the facing putty. Start where you like and feed in little nodules of putty as you proceed around the edge, using the heel of your hand to press it fully home. The finished height of the facing putty must be no higher than the inside level of the frame, and therefore not visible from inside.

Finish the job by trimming off waste putty with a putty knife. Hold the flat edge against the pane of glass and run the knife along the edge of the putty, pressing firmly downwards as you go (fig. 7). If the knife sticks, wet the blade with water. Should the putty become unstuck as you drag the knife over it, push it back in firmly and continue trimming with the knife.

Finally, rake off the putty that has oozed out at the back of the glass level with the frame.

Wooden beading

Some timber windows use wooden beading in place of facing putty (fig. 11) and you can usually use this again when you set the new pane. Remove the side beading first—because it is longer and therefore more flexible—by bowing the ends towards you.

Then remove the small fixing nails afterwards by pulling them right through the beading—do not try to knock them back through the beading as this may split the wood. When you have removed all the nails, clean the beading with a medium grade of glasspaper. Any old putty on the back must be removed, as must the jagged edge left by the broken paint line where the bead joins the frame.

If the old beading is damaged and needs replacing, ask your supplier for *staff beading* in the length required. It is normally available in two sizes, so take along a piece of the old beading.

The mitred joints at the ends of glazing

9 *For a beaded window, start by carefully levering off the wooden beading, especially if this is to be used again for re-glazing*

11 *Push the glass home against the bedding putty. Apply a small amount to the front glass and the nearby framework*

10 *Much the same procedure is used as far as glass and putty removal is concerned. After making good, apply the bedding putty*

12 *Seat the wooden beading on this bedding seal and use small nails to fix the beading tight in place. Trim excess putty*

★ WATCH POINT ★

When painting the glazed window, carry the paint layer just beyond the edges of the putty and on to the glass in order to provide a better waterproof seal and to keep the putty moist.

---

beads are most easily cut on a mitre block. If you do not have one, lay the new length beside the old one and use the latter as a cutting guide. It helps if both are taped or clamped together before cutting.

Beading is positioned as the sheet of glass is pushed home on the bedding putty. Fix

the shorter (top and bottom) lengths first, using nails at 100mm intervals (fig. 12). For a really neat finish, punch in the glazing pins first so that the heads will not be visible when the beading itself is later decorated.

Use the point of a putty knife to remove bedding putty that has oozed out of the back and sides.

Decorating

Leave the freshly bedded putty to mature for about four weeks before you paint it. But do not delay this final job for too long or the putty will shrink and crack, causing all sorts of problems later.

REPAIRING WINDOW FRAMES

A neglected window spoils the appearance of a home, causes draughts and damp, and can tempt intruders. If the signs of decay are not detected and dealt with at an early stage, further deterioration will make repair work more difficult.

Types of window

The two basic types of timber-framed window are the casement sash (fig. C) and the double-hung sliding sash window (fig. B).

The sliding sash window operates by means of cords, pulleys and weights which counterbalance the sashes—the opening parts of the window—as they slide up and down. Two sets of beadings—thin lengths of wood—hold the sashes straight in the frame. Covers or caps in the lower part of the inner edge of the frame are usually provided to allow access to the compartments containing the weights.

A casement window is attached to the frame by hinges and is held open by means of a stay, which is designed to allow progressive adjustment.

Working considerations

The most common problems affecting timber-framed windows are decay from wet rot, loose joints in the sashes and—in the case of sash windows—fraying or broken sash cords. To repair these faults you have to remove the sash so that you can get at the individual components of the window or work on the sash itself—difficult or impossible if it were left standing in the frame.

Where a section of a sash is decayed, you can strengthen it by cutting out and renewing the affected part of the wood. If the joints which hold the sash together are working loose, you can reinforce these by knocking them apart and re-assembling them with fresh adhesive. But if the decay is particularly widespread, rot may have irreparably harmed the timber fibres and the only solution is to discard the sash and fit a new one.

If you have modern casement windows, replacing a decayed section of the casement may be difficult because there is insufficient wood to work with. In this case, it may be quicker and probably more effective to replace the faulty casement altogether.

Above: *Sash cords are fitted into grooves in the side of the sash and held in place by four or five clout nails. Sash cords inevitably fray and need replacing*

If you are dealing with a window affected by rot, it is best to carry out the work during dry weather as the timber remains swollen in damp conditions, making any repairs less than perfect after eventual shrinkage in dry, warm conditions.

Before starting work, identify the type of rot. Wet rot is more common in window frames but you may find dry rot in which case treatment can be more drastic and you should seek expert advice.

Casement window

Older types of casement windows are constructed from thick timber and are therefore heavy. So, if you have to remove the casement for replacement or repair, the work must be tackled with great care.

Begin by passing a strong cord around the window, under the top hinge, and tie this to the upper part of a step ladder to prevent the casement from falling to the ground.

Before you attempt to remove the screws holding the hinges in place, use an old paintbrush to dab a small amount of proprietary paint stripper on any paint around the screw heads.

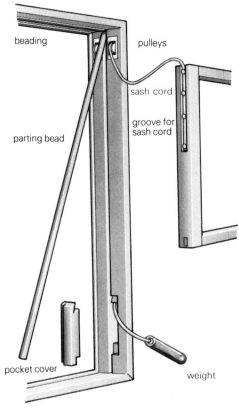

A. *Components of a sash window. The sash cord is nailed to the edge of the sash and tied to a weight*

If the screws prove particularly obstinate and difficult to turn, try to tighten them slightly first to help loosen the threads, or give the end of the screwdriver a few sharp taps with a mallet. If all else fails, apply some penetrating oil and leave it to soak into the screw holes overnight.

Remove the screws which fix the hinges to the frame first—those in the casement are easier and safer to remove once you have taken the window out of the frame. Loosen each of the screws by one full turn and then unscrew two from each hinge, leaving one screw in each.

Now, starting with the upper hinge, remove the remaining screws. Give the casement extra support with one hand under the outer corner and then swing it sideways into the room or, if you are working on the ground floor, lower it to the ground.

Removing a sash window

If a sash window is neglected, it becomes difficult to open and close properly and eventually its cords may fray and snap. To cure these problems, it is usually necessary

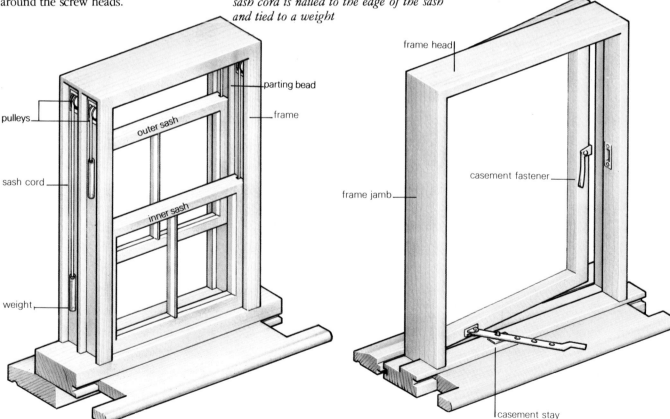

B. *The weights counterbalance the sashes, allowing them to slide up and down. The sashes are held in place by lengths of beading pinned into grooves*

C. *A casement window. The casement is attached to the frame by hinges. A casement stay holds it open and a fastener allows it to be shut tight*

to remove both sashes from the frame.

Start by removing the fixing beads around the inside edge of the frame. Beginning with a long piece, use an old chisel to prise it away starting from the middle of its length. Bring it out to a distance of about 25mm from the frame and then tap it smartly back into place. This should cause the bead's fixing pins to rise up through the surface so that you can remove them with a pair of pincers.

Repeat this procedure for the remaining pieces of beading, then take out the inner, or lower, sash and rest it temporarily on the window sill. Ease the parting bead which runs between the two sashes from its housings then slide out the outer sash.

Sash cords are usually nailed into grooves in the sides of the sashes. To detach the cords of the inner sash, make pencil marks

on the front of each sash to show where the ends of the cords reach to, then make corresponding marks on the outer frame. Afterwards, remove the clout nails which hold the cords in place and—unless you intend to replace the cords—immediately tap the uppermost nails into the edges of the frame to prevent the weights on the other end of the cords from falling down behind the stile boards (fig. 6).

With both cords removed from the inner sash, you can take it from the frame and repeat the procedure for the outer one.

Replacing sash cords

If the frame of a sash window needs attention, it is likely that the sash cords are also in a poor condition and need to be replaced. And if one of the cords has already snapped, it is possible that the others are frayed and about to break, so it is best to replace all four at the same time.

For renewing the cords, buy a slightly longer length of pre-stretched wax cord than you need to allow for waste. You will also need a lump of lead or a large nail to act as a weight for dropping the new cords down into the pockets.

1 *To replace a sash cord, take the sash and parting bead from the frame, then remove the pocket cover to gain access to the weight compartment*

2 *Lay the cover aside, then remove the weight from the compartment and pull the old, decayed sash cord away from the frame*

4 *Tie the new cord to the string, pull this down through the pocket, then tie the end of the cord securely to the original weight*

5 *Pull the free end of the cord so that the weight is raised—25mm for the outer sash or almost to the pulley for the inner one*

7 *Fit the new sash cord into the groove in the edge of the sash and then fix it into place with four or five clout nails*

8 *If the mortise and tenon joints of a sash become loose, remove the sash from the frame so that you can re-assemble the joints*

3 *Tie some string to a small weight such as a nail, then thread this over the pulley wheel and out through the pocket opening*

6 *To hold the weight temporarily in position, half-drive a nail through the cord, securing it to the edge of the frame*

9 *With the glass removed from the sash frame, use a shavehook to scrape away all traces of putty from the timber*

★ WATCH POINT ★

In some windows, the cord may be knotted into a hole in the side of the sash. The method of replacing is much the same, but tying the knot in exactly the right place might require some trial and error.

Remove the sashes from the frame, as described above, and begin work on the cords of the outer sash. To get to the weights to which they are attached, unscrew the pocket covers—or lever them out if they are simply nailed or wedged into place—then pull the weights through the pocket openings and remove the cords.

To fix the first new cord, tie your nail or lead weight to a piece of string about 1.5m long and feed it over the groove of the outer pulley wheel until it falls down behind the stile. Tie the new sash cord to the other end of the string and pull it over the pulley and out through the pocket opening. Now untie the string, secure the cord to the original weight and replace this inside its compartment.

Pull the weight up about 25mm and half-drive a nail through the cord, into the edge of the frame to hold the weight temporarily in position. Cut the cord so that it is level with the pencil mark on the frame, made when you first removed the sashes.

Next position the outer sash so that you can fit the cord into its groove, align the end of the cord with the pencil mark on the front of the sash, then fix the cord in place with four or five clout nails. Repeat the procedure for the other cord, remove the temporary nails and lift the sash back into place within the frame.

The procedure for renewing the cords of the inner sash is almost the same but in this case pull the weights up further, almost to the pulley, before fixing the temporary nails (fig. 5).

Then replace the pocket covers, parting bead, the inner sash and then the outer beading. Grease the channels with a little candle wax to aid smooth running.

Strengthening a sash

If the mortise and tenon joints of a sash become loose, water will eventually penetrate the gaps, causing decay in the sash and possibly the surrounding timber as well. Extensive and costly repairs could

---

then be the result of an initially minor fault. Remove the glazing pins and the glass, then use a shavehook to scrape away all the remaining putty from the edges of the timber (fig. 9).

Now knock the joints apart, using a mallet with a timber offcut to protect the sash, and clean all the old glue from the tenons with wire wool. The joints in sashes are usually reinforced with two small wedges in each mortise to ensure a firm fit. Remove these and clean the inside of the mortises with an old, blunt chisel.

Using the removed wedges as a guide, mark up and cut replacements slightly longer than the originals to allow for trimming. When you have cut all the replacement wedges, coat the tenons with a waterproof woodworking adhesive and slide them into position in the mortises (fig. 12).

★ WATCH POINT ★

Do not be tempted to strengthen a loose-jointed sash simply by filling the gaps. To do the job properly, remove the sash from the frame and chip away the putty holding the glass in place.

Tap them home with a mallet, again protecting the timber with a piece of waste wood, then apply some glue to two of your new wedges. With the angled edge of each wedge facing inwards, tap them into place with the mallet (fig. 13) then trim off the ends with a chisel (fig. 14).

Fit the remaining wedges, and check that the sash frame is square by measuring the diagonals—which should be equal. Cramp the sash with sash cramps or an improvised 'web' cramp (fig. 15). Once the glue has set, you can reglaze the window and rehang the sash.

Renewing decayed timber

If part of a sash is affected by wet rot, make a probe into the wood with a bradawl to check the extent of the damage. Providing the decayed section is small and is spread over no more than half the thickness of the rail, you can cut out the affected wood and replace it with new timber.

Knock apart the joints as described above to remove the rail which needs repair from the rest of the sash frame. Use a combination square to mark a 45° angle at each end of the decayed area. Then mark

10 *Knock the loose mortise and tenon joints apart, making sure that you protect the frame with a piece of waste timber*

11 *Clean all the old glue from the tenons with wire wool, then clean the area in and around the mortises with an old, blunt chisel*

12 *Having made sure that the pin and socket of each joint are clean and dry, coat the tenons with waterproof woodworking adhesive*

13 *Slide the tenons into position, then glue the replacement wedges and fit them into place. Drive them home until the joint is secure*

14 *When the wedges have been fitted firmly into position, trim off their ends with a chisel so that they are flush*

15 *When all the joints have been re-assembled, check that the sash is square, then cramp it using an improvised web cramp*

horizontal lines slightly below the depth of the decayed section on both sides.

Next, secure the timber in a vice and saw down the angled lines to the depth line with a tenon saw. Use a keyhole saw or a jig saw to cut along the depth line and, with the waste wood removed, smooth down the sawn edges with a bevel-edged chisel.

Use the cut piece of wood as a pattern to measure up the replacement timber, then mark the cutting lines.

Angles of 45° are easiest cut using a mitre box to guide the saw blade, but if you do not have one, continue the cutting lines around all the faces of the timber, then secure it in a vice and cut the replacement section. Plane down the sawn edges of the new wood and check its fit in the sash rail. If it is slightly oversize, sand down.

The replacement wood is fixed into place by two or three screws, countersunk below the surface. Drill holes in the new section for these, staggering them slightly, then apply some glue to the underside and angled faces and cramp the section into place. Extend the screw holes into the sash rail to a depth of at least 12mm, drive in the screws and sink their heads below the surface.

When the glue has set, remove the cramp and plane down the surfaces of the new wood until it is flush with the surrounding timber. Afterwards, fill in the screw holes and reassemble the sash, as described above.

Sticking windows

Apart from the faults already described, casements and sashes can stick because of a build-up of old paint or because the timber in the frame swells slightly.

The former problem is easily solved by removing the offending frame, stripping off all the old paint and then repainting. But swelling is a problem which can come and go with the weather. On casement windows, where it occurs most often, swelling can usually be allowed for by adjusting the casement hinges.

Mark the swollen part of the casement and judge whether increasing or decreasing the depth of one of the hinge recesses will bring it away from the window frame.

To increase the depth, pare away 2mm or so of wood from the recess with a sharp chisel. Try the casement for fit again before you start to remove any more.

To decrease the depth, cut a shim of cardboard or thin hardboard to the shape of the recess and fix it in place with a dab of glue. Punch or drill screw holes through the shim then replace the casement.

CHAPTER 4

PLUMBING, DRAINAGE AND CENTRAL HEATING

A dripping tap is not only a noisy nuisance but also the cause of a stained sink and wasteful of water. The cure, however, is simple and quick to effect. Outside, though, it's desirable to keep water flowing—rainwater belongs in the gutter, not pouring down your walls through a faulty system. Repairs are of prime importance. Back inside, the central heating will need to come under your scrutiny to ensure efficient, trouble-free operation

MENDING TAPS

Dripping taps are a source of constant irritation for any household. But for a repair as small as mending a leaking tap, calling in a plumber is an expensive proposition. Since the leak is usually caused by a worn-out or perished washer, one way of solving the problem is to replace the whole tap with a new one of the modern non-drip, washerless type.

A far cheaper way is to learn to mend the tap yourself. Replacement parts cost only pennies and can usually be fitted in a few minutes, once you know how to take the tap apart.

How taps work

Most taps which have washers work in the same basic way: turning the handle raises or lowers a spindle with the rubber or nylon washer on the end in its seating. When the spindle is raised water flows through the seating and out of the spout; when it is lowered, the flow is cut off. But when the washer becomes worn and disintegrates, water can still creep through, irrespective of the position of the spindle. This is what usually causes the tap to drip. If the seals around the moving spindle are worn as well, leaks will also appear around the handle and the outer cover. Because you will have to dismantle the tap to replace either the washer or the seals, it is usually worth doing both jobs at the same time. If fitting new ones fails to cure the drips, the washer seating itself is probably worn. This is a common problem with older taps, especially in hard water areas, and the cure is to regrind the tap seat.

The most common type of household tap is the upright *pillar tap* (fig. A). The *bib-tap* (fig. C) is similar in operation, but fits into the wall above an appliance or on an outside wall. The patented Supatap is a British type of bib-tap incorporating a valve which enables you to complete repairs without having to turn off the water supply. Modern baths and sink units often have a mixer tap with a fixed or a swivelling nozzle. This is really only two pillar taps combined and they are therefore repaired in exactly the same way.

Left: *Dripping taps are not only a noisy nuisance, they can be expensive as well, especially if it is hot water that is gradually leaking away*

Replacing a washer

To replace the washer on a conventional type of tap, start by turning off the water supply to the tap. Turn the tap on fully to drain away any water left in the pipe. Plug the basin, sink or bath to prevent any of the tap components slipping down the plughole.

The assembly which holds the tap washer and the spindle is known as the head. On older taps, it is covered by an outer shield which screws into the tap body. Newer taps have a combined shield and handle which must be removed as one unit.

To remove a conventional shield, make sure that the tap is turned fully on. Loosen the shield with a spanner or a wrench, unscrew it and leave it loose. You can avoid damaging the chrome plating by covering the jaws of whichever tool you are using with a piece of rag.

Modern shield/handles are either simply a push-fit on to the spindle or else are secured in place by a screw through the top. Check the former first by gently pulling the handle upwards (fig. e).

If it stays fast, dig out the plastic cover in the top to expose the securing screw. With this removed, the handle can be pulled off (fig. d).

The next stage is to remove the head. Locate the hexagon nut at the bottom of the assembly and loosen it, again using the wrench or spanner. Unscrew the head from the body of the tap and remove it. At the base, you can see the washer (or what remains of it) seated in its *jumper*.

On older taps the head assembly will be made of brass and the washer will be held in the jumper by a small nut. Loosen this with the pliers, remove the old pieces of washer and put on the new one, maker's name against the jumper.

On newer taps, the entire head is made of nylon and the washer and jumper are combined in one replaceable unit, which slots into the bottom of the assembly. To replace the washer, you simply pull out the old jumper and push in the new one.

Once you have fitted the new washer, you can re-assemble the tap and turn the water supply back on. If the new washer is seated correctly, there will be no drips from the nozzle and you should be able to turn the tap on and off with little effort.

A. Right: *Exploded view of a typical pillar tap showing its components. On older types the washer may be bolted to the jumper plate*

Supataps

When replacing a washer in a Supatap, there is no need to turn off the water supply—this is done automatically by the check-valve inside the tap. To gain access to the washer, hold the handle in one hand while you loosen the gland nut above it with the other. Holding the gland nut and turning in an anticlockwise direction, unscrew the handle from the tap. As you do

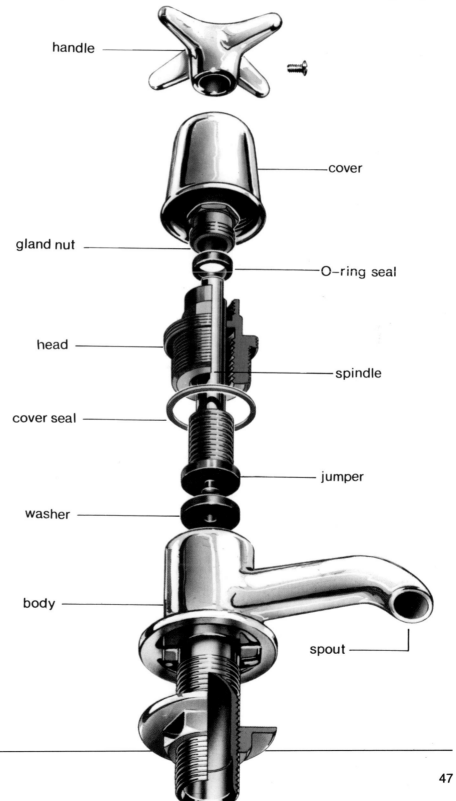

handle

cover

gland nut

O-ring seal

head

spindle

cover seal

jumper

washer

body

spout

1 On this type of tap, remove the cover to expose the securing screw. Undo this and pull the loosened handle upwards to expose the spindle

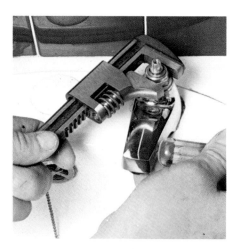

2 When you undo the locking nut, try to wedge the body of the tap against the nearest firm support to avoid undue strain on the pipe

3 Unscrew the head assembly to get at the washer. Check the seating in the tap body for corrosion while the tap is dismantled

4 On some types of tap, the washer is held to its jumper by a small securing nut on the base of the head —undo this with pliers

5 You can then dig out the old washer and replace it. For a temporary repair you can even reverse the old washer

6 To replace the spindle O-ring seals, dig out the circlip holding the spindle to the tap head. Take care not to damage the circlip

7 Once the circlip is loosened, you can slide the spindle out. You can see the various O-rings used on this particular design

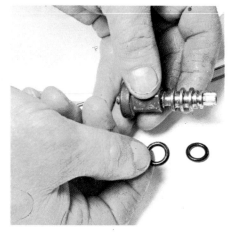

8 If the seals are worn, prise them off with a pin. Slide on new ones and make sure these are properly seated before re-assembling the tap

9 To replace a Supatap washer, start by loosening the locknut above the nozzle assembly. There is no need to turn off the water supply

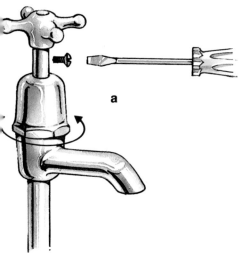

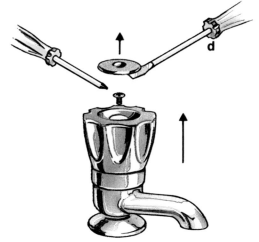

retaining nut like the older type of pillar tap described above.

Leaking spindles

If the leak is coming from around the spindle of the tap rather than the nozzle there are two possible causes. Either the O-ring seal around the spindle has worn out or else the gland nut which holds it is in need of adjustment. Both problems tend to be more common on older taps with brass heads: the newer sort with nylon heads have a better record for remaining watertight.

To service the spindle, you have to

this, there will be a slight rush of water which will stop as soon as the handle is removed and the check-valve drops down.

Protruding from the dismantled handle, you will see the tip of the flow straightener. Push or knock this out on to a table and identify the push-in washer/jumper assembly at one end. Pull off the old washer/jumper and replace it with a new one. Before you re-assemble the tap it is a good idea to clean the flow straightener with a nail brush.

Stop-valve taps

There is normally little difference between a crutch-type stop-valve tap and the more conventional type of pillar tap.

Normally, stop-valve taps have no outer shield and the head is exposed. Loosen the nut securing it with a spanner or wrench and then unscrew the head to expose the washer assembly. Stop-valve washers are usually held in their jumpers with a small

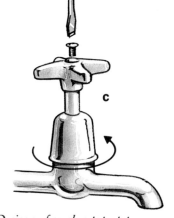

B. *Designs of washer-type taps vary widely, but dismantling procedures will follow one of these: a) old pillar tap, b) Supatap, c) old bib tap, d) and e) new-style pillar taps*

remove the tap handle. On newer types of tap, this may have been done already in order to replace the washer, but on older cross-head taps the handle will still be in place.

Once you have done this, mark the position of the gland nut at the top of the

---

★ WATCH POINT ★

The cross-head will be held on either by a grub screw in the side or by a screw through the top, possibly obscured by a plastic cover. Having undone the screw, you should be able to pull off the handle. If it will not move, turn the tap fully off and unscrew the shield below to force the handle loose.

---

tap head against the head itself with a screwdriver. Next loosen the nut and unscrew it completely. Check the condition of the O-ring or packing around the seating below and, where necessary, replace it. If an O-ring is not available, use string smeared with petroleum jelly.

If the seal around the spindle appears to be in good condition, the leak is probably due to the gland nut above working loose. Replace the nut and tighten it gently so that it just passes the mark that you made against the head. Temporarily replace the handle and check that the tap can be easily turned. If it is too tight, slacken the gland nut. But if, with the water supply turned on, the tap instead continues to leak, then the gland nut will require further tightening to solve the problem.

Taps without gland nuts

Some taps do not have conventional gland nut assemblies, even though their heads are

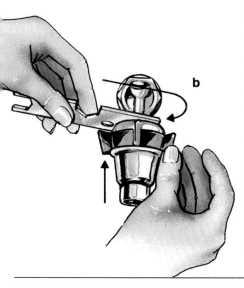

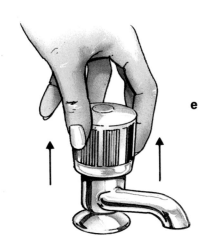

10 *The flow straightener can be knocked out using light taps from a hammer. The washer and its jumper are on the other end*

11 *The combined washer and jumper is prised from the flow straightener and a new one of the same size slotted in its place*

12 *To cure a leaking nozzle, undo the shroud at the base. This either unscrews or may be released by a grub screw at the back*

13 *Pinch together the large circlip at the base. Use pliers for this and take care not to scratch the chromed finish of the nozzle*

14 *Pull the spout from its seat and then dig out the worn seal in the exposed base. Remove all bits before fitting new ones*

15 *Place the replacement seal on the spout before refitting this. Replace the circlip and then screw on the shroud*

made of brass. Instead, the spindle is held in the head by means of a circlip. The seal between them is provided by two or more O-rings around the spindle body, and if these are worn they must be replaced. Follow the procedures above for removing the tap handle and unscrewing the head. Prise out the circlip around the top of the spindle as shown in fig. 6 and you will find that the spindle drops out. The O-rings around it can then be easily rolled off and replaced.

Leaking swivel nozzles

Mixer taps with swivelling spouts are often

★ WATCH POINT ★

If you find you have to make a temporary repair to a tap seating—a very necessary exercise if dripping continues even when the defective washer has been removed and replaced—try using a new plastic washer and seating kit.

---

prone to leaks around the base of the spout itself, caused by the seals in the base wearing out. Providing you are working on the spout alone, it will not be necessary to turn off the water. Start by loosening the

shroud around the base, which will either be a type that screws on or one that is secured by a small grub screw situated at the back.

Around the spout, inside the base, you will find a large circlip. Pinch this together with the pliers and remove it, then pull out the spout.

Dig the worn seals out of the exposed base and discard them. Fit the new ones around the spout: if you fit them into the base, you will have great difficulty in getting the spout to go back in the correct position. With the seals around the spout it should slot back into place quite easily and you can then neatly replace the circlip and the shroud in position.

REPAIRING GUTTERS

Gutters and downpipes play a vital role in protecting your house from the effects of rain, but if they are to work properly they must be regularly checked for blockages, cracks and leaks. Even if they show no obvious signs of damage, you should still make a point of inspecting your gutters and downpipes once, or preferably twice, each year.

You will find that leaves and debris accumulate in the gutters, particularly during the autumn months, and if you don't clear this out, you could end up with a blocked downpipe. If left, blockages allow water to flow over the edge of the gutter and down into the wall of a house to cause penetrating damp.

Basic maintenance

Clear out the rubbish with a hand brush and trowel or, in the case of plastic guttering, with a piece of hardboard shaped to fit the curve of the guttering and attached to a piece of wood. Try to keep the debris well away from the downpipe outlet.

If you have cast-iron guttering, check carefully for signs of rust. Use a wire brush to remove loose flakes of paint and rust and treat the surface with a proprietary rust-inhibiting chemical. Ideally, you should follow up with one or two coats of bituminous paint to form a strong, protective surface.

Ogee-section guttering is often attached directly to the fascia, rather than held in brackets. Here, rust is most likely to be

Above: *Debris soon accumulates in gutters if they are often left unattended. Cleaning them out is an easy and worthwhile task*

found around the fixing screws. The affected section must be removed and refixed with galvanized screws.

Leaking joints

Next check the joints for leaks: cast-iron gutters are particularly prone to this. A quick and easy remedy is to apply mastic to the defective joint. This is only a temporary repair, however, and the joint should be undone and resealed as soon as possible.

Resealing metal joints

Sections of cast-iron guttering are held together by a nut and a bolt with a wide, slotted head. A proprietary sealing compound (often a mixture of putty and red

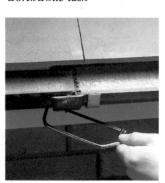

1 *If the bolt has completely rusted up, you'll have to cut it off with the help of a hacksaw*

2 *Try to get off all the old pieces of sealant that still remain on the gutter section before you actually start to reassemble the joint again*

3 *You can use mastic or putty to seal the joint—don't skimp with how much you use; you can always clear off any excess*

4 *Use a spanner to hold the nut firmly in place as you screw the new, replacement bolt right through the piece of guttering*

5 *As you tighten the bolt, putty will start to ooze out—you can scrape off the excess with the aid of a putty knife*

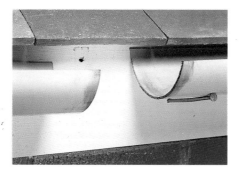

6 *Support the guttering while the bracket is removed—nails will easily take all the weight*

7 *Clean off the ends of both sections of guttering—petrol is very useful to remove particles of rubber*

8 *Reassemble the joint and then snap the bracket back into position around the guttering*

lead, or a mastic sealer) is sandwiched between the ends of adjoining sections to make the joint watertight. If a joint starts to leak, one of the sections will have to be removed, and the ends of both parts cleaned thoroughly and resealed. If the section you need to remove comes in the middle of a run, you'll have to undo and reseal the joints at both ends of it.

Start by removing the bolt which holds the joint together. If this has rusted and seized, try applying some penetrating oil. If this fails, saw through the bolt with a junior hacksaw (fig. 1), then lift out the loosened section and take it to ground level.

Chip away all traces of old sealing compound from the ends of both sections of guttering and scour them thoroughly with a wire brush. Apply fresh sealing compound to the socket section of the joint, spreading it in an even layer about 6mm thick and re-assemble the joint. Fit a new bolt through the hole from above and screw on the securing nut. Tighten up with a screw-driver and spanner until the joint closes completely and the sealing compound begins to squeeze out.

Scrape away the excess sealing compound from both the face and underside of the gutter (fig. 5).

Resealing plastic joints

Nearly all new houses are fitted with lightweight plastic guttering which will not rust and is much cheaper and easier to replace if you do have problems.

Sections of plastic guttering are connected by union clips lined with replaceable rubber seals. In some cases, the seal is positioned in the end of one section of gutter with a separate clip used to secure the joint. When the clip is sprung home, the gutter ends compress the seal to form a watertight joint. However, if silt finds its way in the seal may leak and have to be cleaned out or a new seal fitted.

To do this, release the clip by pulling the lip at the back over the gutter edge and squeezing the front edge. Peel off the old seal. If particles of perished rubber stick to the clip, you can remove this with petrol. Remember, too, to clean the face and underside of the two end sections of gutter. After cleaning, fit the new seal, then squeeze the ends of the gutter slightly and snap on the union clip back over each edge.

Some systems use a combined union and bracket, with these a silt bridge is fitted into the union to ensure that grit and dirt cannot

get between the union and the gutter. Leaks in this type of joint are usually caused by cracks either in the bridge or the union bracket and can be remedied by replacing the defective part.

Start by removing and examining the silt bridge. If this is free of cracks, you need to unscrew the union bracket—but make sure the gutter is supported by nails driven into the fascia before you do so. Ease the ends of both sections of gutter out of the union bracket, clean both the surface and under-side of the ends of each section.

Secure the new bracket to the fascia—use longer screws if the holes have become enlarged—and refit the silt bridge by hooking one end under the front of the bracket, then snapping the other end under the lip at the back of the gutter.

Clearing a downpipe

Before you attempt to clear a blocked downpipe, first put a plastic bowl under the base of the pipe at the discharge into the drain to prevent any debris being pushed further into the drainage system.

If the downpipe is fitted with a hopper head, carefully clear by hand any debris

9 *Start by clearing the loose debris out of the hopper head—try not to push it down*

10 *Tackle the blockage with a suitable implement to try to clear it*

11 *Finally flush the pipe with water—a garden hose is ideal if it will reach*

12 *An offcut of wood will make it easier to lever away fixings*

which has collected. Try not to push any waste down or it could cause a more serious blockage (fig. 9).

With plastic hopper heads, wipe the inside with a cloth and soapy water once the rubbish has been cleared. And when clearing a cast-iron hopper head wear rubber gloves to protect your hands from any rough edges.

If you are dealing with a straight downpipe, try poking it clear with a piece of wire.

A. *A swan neck makes it slightly more difficult to clear a blockage—try using stiff wire*

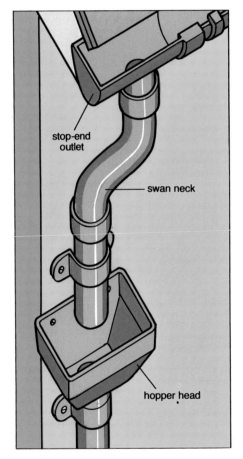

stop-end outlet

swan neck

hopper head

If this doesn't work, try washing it out with a garden hose. For a really stubborn blockage, you can use a flexible wire drain rod, which can be fed up or down and rotated to shift the debris. In the absence of one of these, tie a rag firmly to one end of a long pole and poke it down the pipe (fig. 10). Once the blockage has been dislodged, flush the pipe thoroughly with water (fig. 11).

With some systems, the guttering is positioned some way out from the wall and water is directed into the downpipe through an angled section known as a *swan neck* (fig. A). To clear a blockage here, use a length of fairly stiff wire.

If you are dealing with a downpipe on a two- or three-storey house and the blockage is situated close to the bottom of the pipe, you may not be able to clear it using a long pole. In this case, you will have to start removing the bottom sections of downpipe until you trace where the blockage lies. To do this, follow the same procedure used when dealing with a loose downpipe bracket.

Once you've cleared the debris and reassembled the pipe, make sure you fit a grille over the downpipe outlet and regularly clear out hopper heads and gutters to prevent the same thing from happening in the future.

Securing a loose downpipe

Downpipes are secured to the wall by brackets which are held in place by pipe nails—long round-headed nails driven into metal, lead or wooden plugs bedded into the brickwork. If the pipe is inadequately secured it is under stress and there is a risk of it breaking—particularly if it is made of cast-iron.

To refit the loose bracket, you will need to remove any brackets which are fitted

underneath it, starting with the one nearest the ground, and also remove the section of pipe.

Place an offcut of timber against the wall to give you enough leverage to remove the nails holding the bracket in place, then remove the section of downpipe and lay it aside. Repeat the procedure until you reach the defective bracket.

Once you have removed the loose bracket, dig out the old plugs from the masonry and make up replacements which are slightly larger than the existing holes. Cut these from a piece of 12mm dowel, then extend the holes using a 12mm

masonry drill bit. Drive in the replacement plugs until they are flush with the wall, replace the last section of downpipe removed, and refit the bracket. Repeat this procedure moving downwards, replacing any plugs which have become loose. Before you start replacing the sections, check each one thoroughly for rust and renew them if necessary.

Plastic downpipes are much lighter and the securing brackets are less likely to become loose. If they do, however, follow the same procedure—working from the base of the pipe upwards—to reach the defective bracket. Sections of plastic downpipe are joined by a socket and spigot type of connector and there is no need to seal the joints.

13 *If the pipe won't separate, heat the joint to melt the old sealant*

14 *Take care when removing the section of downpipe—it is heavy*

15 *Hammer the new plug into the masonry—use the old plugs if they feel secure*

16 *When the joint is re-assembled, scrape off any excess sealant*

CENTRAL HEATING PROBLEMS

When a central heating system ceases to function properly, it becomes an expensive liability. But it does not always take an expert to repair it. Many common faults can be cured just as easily by the householder.

The most complicated part of the average domestic central heating system is the boiler. This may require specialist knowledge and tools to put it right should it fail—but failures in boilers which are regularly serviced are rare. More prone to trouble are circulation pumps, thermostats and radiators.

Faults here are usually easy to identify and even if a specialist has to be called in, being able to pinpoint a problem will help keep repair bills to a minimum.

Wet central heating systems

In order to identify a particular fault in a central heating system, it is worth having some idea of how the system works.

In most modern systems, hot water flows from the boiler to the radiators and hot water cylinder, releases its heat and returns to be reheated. The flow is created artificially by an electric circulation pump which is normally mounted adjacent to the boiler. The pump is controlled by a time clock and, in most cases, by a room thermostat as well.

At pre-selected times, the mechanism in the clock switches on the pump. The pump then sends hot water to the radiators, heating the house.

Maintenance of the system

Although all central heating systems should be serviced at least once a year by qualified engineers, you can keep the system running reliably by correct use and regular maintenance.

It is not advisable to switch off heating at night during cold weather. A small amount of heat—to ensure that the temperature throughout the house never falls below 10°C (50°F)—cuts the time needed to reach full operating temperature and may, in the long run, save fuel. It will also help to reduce condensation and prevent frost damage to the system.

The boiler should never be run at too low a thermostat setting. There is no economic advantage to be gained and it can shorten

Above: *A central heating system is a great asset to a home, but it needs to be regularly serviced and maintained*

★ WATCH POINT ★

Once or twice a year, the circulation pump valves and all the radiator valves should be turned as far as they will go in both directions and then back to their original setting. This will prevent them becoming fixed.

---

the life of the boiler. The boiler thermostat in a conventional small bore system should be set at up to 82°C (180°F) in winter. In summer, when the system is required for hot water only, it should be kept at not less than 54°C (130°F).

If the system is oil-fired, the oil tank should be examined annually. Any external rust should be removed with a wire brush and glasspaper and then painted over with black bitumen paint. Keep the vent pipe on top of the tank clear, removing any obstruction with a stiff piece of wire. A piece of fine wire mesh can be fitted over the end of the vent pipe to ensure that leaves do not enter the tank and restrict the flow of fuel to the boiler.

To clean the oil filter on an oil tank, turn off the stop cock and remove the filter bowl. Clean the element with paraffin, dry it and refit. At the same time check the oil line

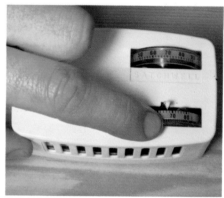

1 *To check a room thermostat, turn it to its lowest setting. Turn it back up again, listening for a click as the pump is switched on*

5 *To free an air lock in the pump, unscrew the vent valve located at the top. When water begins to trickle out, close the valve*

from the tank to the boiler for leaks, tightening joints where necessary.

When a solid fuel boiler is not in use it should be left clean. Remove sooty deposits from the combustion chamber and flue and leave the damper and boiler doors open to allow a current of air to pass through. Have the flue cleaned at least once a year.

If a central heating system has to be left drained for any length of time and stop valves are fitted on either side of the circulation pump, you can close the valves, remove the pump and dry it thoroughly to prevent rusting.

Overheating

Overheating is one of the most common faults found in wet central heating systems. In all cases of overheating, if the fault cannot be rectified at once, the supply of gas or oil to the boiler should be cut off as a precaution. If you can run the circulation pump with the boiler off, keep it circulating water so that the heat is dissipated through the radiators. With a solid fuel boiler, rake the fire into the ashpan and remove it.

If the house feels abnormally hot, check the time clock and, if there is one, the room thermostat. These may be failing to turn the pump off when they should or have had their settings accidentally advanced. Start by turning the time clock down to the present setting. If the radiators do not cool

---

★ WATCH POINT ★

To find out whether the pump is working, hold one end of a screwdriver against the casing with the other end to your ear and listen for the hum of the rotor inside (fig. 2): if there is no noise, this is probably stuck.

---

down at the time they are supposed to, the mechanism of the clock has probably jammed and will have to be replaced with a new one.

To check a room thermostat, turn it down to its lowest setting and then back up again. A click should be heard as the switch inside turns the pump on. If there is no click, the unit will have to be replaced.

If the whole system is overheating seriously, the radiator pipes may make prolonged knocking or hissing noises and there will be excessive temperature in the boiler delivery pipe. One possible reason for this is failure of the circulation pump.

On pumps with a screw-on glass inspection cover, the rotor can be freed quite easily. Turn the pump off, unscrew the cover and insert a screwdriver into one of the slots in the rotor. If the rotor does not spin freely, it should be possible to free it by levering gently with the screwdriver (fig. 4).

On pumps which have all metal casings, the water supply must be cut off before

2 *To find out whether a circulation pump is working, hold one end of a screwdriver against the casing with the handle to your ear*

3 *On pumps with all-metal casings, you may have to drain the system and remove the unit before you can unscrew the casing*

4 *If the rotor has seized, you may be able to free it by inserting a screwdriver into one of the slots and levering gently*

6 *To check the boiler thermostat, turn the dial down and then back to its maximum setting. If there is no click, the thermostat is jammed*

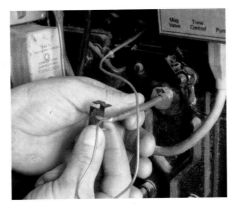

7 *If the sender bulb on the end of the copper capillary has come out of place, reposition it and replace its securing clip*

8 *Make sure that the level of water in the expansion tank is not more than 150mm from the valve outlet. If it is, add more water*

opening the cover. In most cases, there are stop valves on each side for this purpose but where no such valves are fitted, the system will have to be drained before carrying out any work on the pump.

If the pump is heard to be working but water is evidently not circulating, there is probably an air lock. At the top of the pump you will find a vent valve—operated either by a key or a screwdriver—from which the pump can be bled (fig. 5).

To do this, turn the pump off and leave it for a few hours to allow the water in the system to settle. Then open the valve to bleed off the air. A hiss of air will be followed by a trickle of water: when the trickle becomes constant, you can close off the valve.

If the fault is not in the pump, the boiler thermostat may have failed. The thermostat, a small box with a dial on the top, is located behind the boiler casing. Remove the casing and check that the electrical connections on the thermostat are sound. Check also that the sender bulb on the end of the copper capillary from the thermostat to the boiler has not fallen out of its socket (fig. 7). If so, reposition it and replace the securing clip.

Note the setting on the boiler thermostat dial and turn it down low. After a few minutes turn it back towards its maximum setting and listen for a click. If there is no click, it may mean that the thermostat has become jammed and you should call in a qualified engineer to give it a thorough maintenance check.

If the boiler thermostat appears to be working, check to see whether the boiler flue outlet outside has become blocked in some way. Depending on the nature of the blockage, expert help may be needed in order to clear it.

If the flue is free of any obstruction, the next thing to check is the expansion tank. The ball valve supplying it may have become jammed or seized, in which case there may not be enough water in the system to absorb the heating action of the boiler. If the level in the tank is more than 150mm from the valve outlet, free the valve and introduce more water into the system. Where the valve is completely seized, replace it with a new ballcock, arm and piston unit.

Central heating too cool

If all the radiators are cool and the boiler is working correctly, the fault probably lies with one of the thermostats, the time clock

or the circulation pump. Carry out checks outlined above under 'Overheating', paying special attention to the position of a room thermostat if fitted. This reacts to the temperature around it, and a nearby heat source can cause it to give a false reading even though the mechanism may be perfectly sound.

To work efficiently, the thermostat should be mounted on an internal wall at least 1.5m above the floor and away from draughts, radiators and direct sunlight. It should not be placed in rooms which are in constant use—such as lounges—because people generate extra heat, nor in kitchens, because of the heat from cooking and appliances. However, it should be accessible so that changes in setting can be made conveniently.

Draining the system

Before doing any major repairs or modifications to your central heating, you will have to drain, or partially drain, the system. Start by turning the boiler off and leaving the system for a few hours to cool down. Turn off the electricity supply to the time clock and the immersion heater—if the system includes one (fig. 9).

Shut off the water supply to the boiler by closing the stop valve on the pipe into the expansion tank (fig. 10). If no stop valve is fitted to the system, lash the ball valve in the expansion tank to a piece of wood laid across the tank.

When the system has cooled, return to the boiler and identify the main drain cock. This is usually at the front end of the boiler near the pump where it is always built into the lowest pipe. Alternatively, it may be found on a ground-floor radiator. Attach one end of a garden hose to the nozzle and run the other to an outside drain. Open the drain cock by turning the nut beneath with a spanner or adjustable wrench and allow as much water as you require to drain away (fig. 12).

Refilling the system

Before refilling, close the main drain cock securely. Open the valve on the pipe leading to the expansion tank, or untie the ball valve, to admit fresh water into the system. Regulate the position of the valve so that the tank fills slowly—keeping the risk of air locks to a minimum. Also check the drain cock for leaks.

9 *Before draining a central heating system, turn off the electricity supply to the time clock and also to the immersion heater, if fitted*

12 *Run the other end of the hose to an outside drain, then open the drain cock by turning the nut beneath with an adjustable wrench*

15 *Metal pipe brackets are another common source of noise. Bend them back slightly and stuff pieces of felt into the gaps*

10 *To shut off the water supply to the boiler, close the stop valve tap on the pipe which leads into the expansion tank*

11 *When the system has cooled down, attach one end of a garden hose to the nozzle of the main drain cock on the boiler*

13 *Pipes often creak where they run through a notch in a floor joist. Cushion the pipes with felt or carpet to stop the noise*

14 *A pipe may rub against wood where it rises through the floor. Pack the gap round the pipe with pieces of suitable padding*

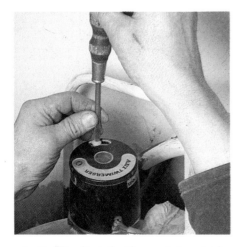

16 *To adjust the thermostat control of an immersion heater, unscrew the element cover on the top or side of the cylinder*

17 *Remove the cover to locate the temperature dial. Turn the dial by hand or with a screwdriver to the desired temperature mark*

Noise

Noise is another common problem with wet central heating systems. Creaking under the floorboards and around radiators is caused by pipes—which expand and contract according to the temperature of the water—rubbing against the floor joists on which they rest. Creaking can also occur where a pipe rises through the floorboards to feed a radiator.

If the noise persists, take up the floorboards around the suspect area. Eventually you will find a point where one or two pipes cross a joist and are notched into the woodwork. If the notch is so small that it causes the pipes to rub against each other, enlarge it to give a better clearance. Make sure, though, that the notch does not exceed one sixth of the depth of the joist or it will seriously weaken the timber. Use a piece of rubber pipe lagging, felt or carpet, trimmed to the approximate size of the notch, to cushion the pipes (fig. 13).

Where a pipe rises through a gap in a floorboard, either enlarge the gap by filing it away or pack the space around the pipe with padding (fig. 14). Metal pipe brackets—another common source of noise—can be bent back slightly, and stuffed with felt to prevent them making direct contact with the pipes (fig. 15).

Creaking behind radiators is usually caused by the hooks on the back of the panels rubbing against their corresponding wall brackets. For serious cases, on smaller radiators, special nylon brackets can be fitted in place of the normal pressed steel type. A simpler solution is to place pieces of felt or butyl rubber between each hook and bracket. This can be done, with the help of an assistant, by gently lifting the radiator away from its brackets, slipping the pieces of felt into the hooks and then replacing it.

Immersion heaters

In many systems, hot water for sinks and baths is heated by a thermostatically controlled immersion heater in addition to the boiler-fed heat exchanger. The thermostat is pre-set to turn the heating element off when the water reaches the selected temperature. If the water is unbearably hot, the thermostat may simply need adjusting.

The thermostat control is found at the top or on the side of the hot water cylinder (fig. 16). To adjust it, turn off the electricity supply to the heater then unscrew the element cover where you will find a small

dial marked centigrade, fahrenheit, or both. By hand, or with a screwdriver, turn the regulator screw to the desired temperature—normally 60°C (140°F) in hard water areas or 80°C (180°F) in those with especially soft water.

If the water heats up slowly, or the hot tap cools too quickly, check that the cylinder is sufficiently lagged and that the lagging is in good condition. If it is, try adjusting the thermostat. When water fails to heat up at all, either the thermostat control or the heating element is defective and will have to be replaced.

Radiator controls

Most radiators are fitted with two valves—a *handwheel* and a *lockshield* valve. The handwheel allows radiators to be shut down individually or the temperature of a radiator to be reduced by restricting the flow of water. The lockshield valve is set when the system is installed, to give a balanced flow of water through the radiator.

★ WATCH POINT ★

Creaking from the radiators can often be reduced by turning the boiler thermostat down so that the radiators remain switched on for longer periods instead of constantly heating up and cooling down.

Above: *Most radiators are fitted with two valves, called a handwheel and a lockshield valve, which control the flow of water*

There is no basic difference between the two valves except that the lockshield valve is locked into position to prevent casual adjustment. A lockshield valve should normally need adjusting only when a radiator has to be removed for decoration or repair. When this is necessary, both the lockshield valve and the handwheel should be closed. To close a lockshield valve, unscrew the cover and turn the valve with a spanner or a wrench.

In some cases, thermostatic radiator valves are fitted in place of handwheels. A radiator thermostat can be pre-set to maintain any desired temperature and is controlled by temperature-sensitive bellows. As the water temperature falls, the bellows contract to allow more hot water into the radiator. Radiator thermostats are usually only suitable for use in a two-pipe type of system.

Bleeding a radiator

When air accidentally enters a wet central heating system, it can find its way to a radiator and prevent this from functioning

Right: *To bleed a radiator, undo the valve screw and release the trapped air until water spurts out*

efficiently. All radiators should be bled of air once or twice a year to clear the small amounts that inevitably get into the system. But if a radiator becomes cold while others are functioning normally, the cause is probably a substantial air lock and the radiator should be bled immediately. The top of a radiator remaining cold while the bottom is scalding also suggests an air lock.

On most radiators a square-ended hollow key—obtainable from ironmongers—is needed to open the air vent valve at the top. To prevent air being sucked into the system, turn down the room thermostat and switch off the time clock so that the pump stops working.

Place a towel underneath the radiator to catch any drips, then open the valve by turning the key anticlockwise until a hiss of escaping air is heard. As soon as water begins to flow, re-tighten the valve.

If air locks occur frequently in a certain radiator, you can fit a screw bleed valve or an automatic air eliminator. These save you the nuisance of constantly having to bleed it by hand.

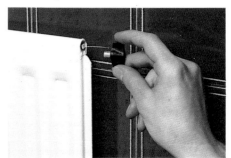

CHAPTER 5

HOME FURNISHINGS

Once you've tackled the major repairs to your property, don't assume that your job is over. Your furniture, furnishings and ornaments are susceptible to damage by accidents at any time—and most at risk are your carpets. With care, invisible patches can be applied. Furniture that's past its best can be given a bright new look with a number of treatments, while even your favourite shattered china and porcelain can be carefully repaired thanks to today's efficient adhesives

RENOVATING FURNITURE

By stripping old furniture down to the natural wood you can ensure a smooth surface—free of bumps and blemishes—which can then be polished, varnished or even stencilled for a completely new look.

Make sure, though, that you know what finish you are stripping. It could be one of several—paint, polish, lacquer or varnish —and they all need different treatments.

Stripping paint

Paint on furniture can be removed either by immersion in a caustic bath—a job for a specialist—or by hand, using a chemical paint stripper or an electric hot air stripper. Hand stripping usually gives the best results, as it adds an extra lustre to the bare wood.

Liquid strippers

To strip the paint you need a supply of proprietary paint stripper. Available in either jelly or liquid form, it is more economical to buy it by the gallon than to opt for one of the smaller cans. The back of the can should tell you what to wash the stripper off with once it has lifted the paint film—either water, methylated spirits or turps substitute.

To apply the stripper, you need an old 25mm or 50mm paintbrush. For peeling away the softened paint, use a stripping knife and a shavehook or coarse wire wool.

Applying the chemical

If you are working indoors, ensure the room is well ventilated before you start—paint stripper gives off unpleasant fumes. Put down some newspaper or an old dust sheet to protect your floor and furnishings.

On a chest of drawers start with the drawer faces themselves, removing handles and key escutcheons where possible. A dab of paint stripper, left to soak for a few minutes, will help loosen stubborn screws.

Wearing rubber gloves, pour some of the stripper into a jar and start brushing it on to the paint. Work the stripper into all the cracks and crevices, making sure none of the paint is missed.

Having covered a drawer or the equivalent area, leave the stripper to act for several minutes. When the paint starts to bubble, remove the top layer with a stripping knife and scrape the shreds straight into a container such as a jam jar or empty paint tin.

Continue this process with each layer of paint—sometimes there are as many as five or six on an old chest of drawers—until you reach the wood. You will need several applications of stripper. If you find any corners difficult to reach with a stripping knife, use the shavehook instead.

When all the paint has been stripped off, the next step is to wash down the wood. This will help to remove any remaining debris and also neutralizes the stripper.

Follow the manufacturer's recommenda-

tion on what neutralizer to use with your particular stripper. Soak it into a hand-sized wad of wire wool and thoroughly rub over the stripped surfaces. If water is the recommended neutralizer, use copious quantities.

Finally, when the wood is dry, smooth it with glasspaper. Use medium grade paper to work out the deeper scratches, then go over the whole surface with a fine grade. Rub in the direction of the wood grain when using wire wool or glasspaper.

Paste strippers

If you're stripping a large area, a stripping paste is a good method—you coat the whole surface, then peel off the stripper and the old finish together. It's simple to use and very effective in lifting off many coats at once.

This product comes ready mixed in tubs or in powder form—mix it with water in an old bucket and leave it to stand. When making up the paste, wear protective gloves and don't inhale the fumes.

Apply the paste with a trowel, stripping knife or an old brush to a thickness of at least 3mm, making sure there are no air bubbles. Leave for the recommended time, periodically dabbing down the bubbles to keep the stripper in contact with the old finish.

When it is dry, lift a starting edge by prising up a corner of the paste layer with a stripping knife or trowel.

Strip off the paste in layers. Any residues should come off by scrubbing down with a stiff brush and water. 'Kill' the final coat of stripper by washing down the surface with methylated spirit and medium wire wool (00 grade) then with 000 grade wool.

Go over the whole surface with clean water and leave to dry out thoroughly.

Hot air stripping

You can use an electric hot air stripper for fast removal of paint from large items of furniture. Don't, however, use a blowtorch or you'll scorch the wood. To use the stripper, simply play the hot jet over the paint surface and scrape it off when it bubbles. Remember, however, to keep the jet moving all the time to prevent scorching the wood.

Opposite: *A neglected old chest (inset) can easily be stripped down to the natural wood and then polished with a home-made beeswax polish*

Stripping polish

If the chest of drawers is polished you need to know which type of polish has been used before you can remove it successfully.

French polish gives a fine, mirror-like surface which is very delicate and easily marked by heat or liquid. The surface shine is the result of the polishing techniques rather than the ingredients of the polish.

French polish can easily be removed with

★ WATCH POINT ★

The paste must stay moist as it works. If it starts to dry out before the surface has lifted—test a small area to see—wrap the furniture with polythene to hold in the moisture.

1 *Remove the handles from drawers if possible. Pour some stripper into a jar and apply it to the wood. Work it well into any cracks*

3 *Use a moulding scraper to get the paint out of difficult corners and continue applying stripper until all the paint has been removed*

methylated spirits. Wipe it on generously and then leave it for a few minutes. When the polish has softened scrape it off, first with a scraper, then with fine wire wool soaked in methylated spirits. When the wood is dry, glasspaper it down to a smooth finish.

Wax polish and oily surfaces can be removed by rubbing with fine steel wool soaked in turpentine or turps substitute. Dry with an absorbent rag and repeat the process until you reach bare wood.

If you are not sure what sort of polish is on your furniture, choose a small, unobtrusive part of the surface and rub real turpentine on the spot with a soft cloth. This will remove dirt and wax or oil finishes and quickly reveal bare wood. If there is polish left after applying the turpentine, rub on a little methylated spirit—if the surface has been French polished it will go soft and be very sticky.

2 *Leave it until the paint starts to bubble then, with a stripping knife, remove the top layer of paint. Scrape the paint shreds into a tin*

4 *Rub the bare wood with coarse wire wool dampened in turps substitute or water. When dry, rub with glasspaper to smooth it*

Varnished finishes

If your chest of drawers is more than 30 years old and is varnished, you are dealing with oil-based varnish. This is made from resins dissolved in oils and solvents and is quite different from modern varnishes.

The cleanest way to remove oil-based varnish is with a carpenter's cabinet scraper—a cheap tool consisting of a rectangle of metal with one sharp edge. Tilt the scraper away from you and push it along the grain of the wood, working away from your body. Never use it across the grain.

To remove polyurethane varnishes use paint stripper or a proprietary varnish stripper. Cellulose-based varnishes can be removed with paint-stripper, acetone, cellulose thinners, ammonia, caustic soda or turpentine. You may need to test small areas first to see which works best.

Making repairs

Once you have stripped off all the old paint, you may find that various faults show up and that repairs are necessary before the new finish can be applied.

If the back of the chest of drawers is weak, nail some new battening on.

Any weak joints should be glued, pinned, then held in place for several hours—either with string or in a clamp. Make sure that the corners of the chest of drawers are protected from the cutting action of the string with some paper or a piece of wood.

Cracks and holes must be filled with plastic wood or a commercial non-shrinking stopper—both are available from do-it-yourself shops. You can also buy coloured fillers and stains to match the natural colour of the wood. Level filled holes with fine glasspaper.

Large holes, greater than the size of a keyhole, should be plugged with a piece of similar wood cut to shape. Make sure that the grain of the plug goes the same way as the rest of the surface, then glue it in place with a suitable adhesive.

Finishing—with polyurethane

Polyurethane varnish gives bare wood a lustrous, hard-wearing finish which is easy to clean and maintain. As well as clear varnish, a wide variety of colours and natural wood shades are available. The clear varnishes come in matt, gloss and coloured varieties.

Apply the varnish directly to the sanded wood with a paintbrush. Because the varnish must be applied in coats, it is a good idea to dilute the first with white spirit so it soaks in and seals the wood. When the first

5 *Grate the beeswax, using a cheese grater, to help it melt. Then put the wax in a jam jar and add enough turpentine to cover it*

6 *Stand the jam jar in a saucepan of very hot water and then stir the mixture until it all melts and forms a thick paste*

coat is dry, lightly rub it down with fine glasspaper before applying the next. Subsequent coats can be diluted in the proportion of one part white spirit to three parts polyurethane to give thinner coats which will brush on more easily.

Before applying the coloured variety apply one coat of clear polyurethane to seal the wood or you may get a patchy effect. For a matt finish, apply a final coat of clear, matt polyurethane after the coloured coats.

Finishing—with wax polish

Wax polish can either be used in conjunction with polyurethane, or by itself as an alternative finish. Although wax gives a warm, mellow look to the wood, it has hardly any resistance to heat and marks easily—so its use should be confined to more decorative furniture.

With polyurethane, use a proprietary, white wax polish. After the final coat of varnish has dried, rub over it lightly with a very fine (0000) grade of wire wool. Having

7 *Put some of the beeswax polish on a rag and rub it into the surface of the wood. Finish it off with a dry, clean cloth*

8 *If using a polyurethane finish, this can be applied directly on to the stripped wood. For the first coat, dilute the varnish with white spirit*

Left: *Stencil kits are available from art and craft shops or stationers. You will also need sticky tape, chalk, a palette knife, cardboard, a stencil brush, small cans of gloss paints and white spirit*

brushed away the dust, rub in the polish with a coarse rag to give an even, matt sheen.

Finally, buff up the surface with a fine cloth. Successive layers of polish, built up at the rate of one every two days, will deepen and harden the finish.

For a pure wax finish, you can make up your own beeswax polish. For this you need pure beeswax—available from hardware shops—turps substitute and a glass jar. Grate the beeswax with a cheese grater and put it in a jam jar. Pour in just enough turps to cover the wax. Stand the jar in a pan of very hot water and stir until the mixture melts and forms a thick paste—on no account expose the jar to a naked flame as the turps substitute is highly inflammable.

Dip a clean rag in the wax and rub the mixture into the clean wood surface, taking care to spread the wax evenly. Apply enough wax to soak into the grain but avoid leaving any proud of the surface.

When the wax has hardened completely—in about an hour—buff up the surface with a fine cloth to give a mirror finish.

★ WATCH POINT ★

If you want a final matt finish, start with one or two coats of gloss and make only the top coat matt. This gives a much harder-wearing finish.

Above: *A dark background shows off brightly coloured stencils to the full*
Below: *More subdued designs add a touch of prettiness to this cupboard*

Using stencils

Cut out your chosen stencils on a flat surface such as a board, securing them with tape or drawing pins before you begin cutting out the patterns.

Mix your chosen colours with a knife, using a sheet of cardboard as a palette. Fasten the stencil to the wood with clear tape, rub off the chalk and use the stencil brush to daub paint through—or if the area of the stencil is fairly large use a spray can (of enamel, not car paint).

With practice, you can grade colours by lightly applying a contrasting colour over the first colour at the edges of the stencil. Wait until the paint is almost dry before painting adjacent designs or you may smudge the first ones. If you make a mistake, the paint can be removed with white spirit while it is still wet.

When you have finished, clean each stencil with white spirit.

CARPET REPAIRS

A carpet usually covers such a wide area of a room that it is painfully obvious when any part of it becomes damaged, stained or worn. But this everyday, minor damage need not be the disaster you might at first imagine. Most of it can, with care and patience, be repaired to a highly professional standard. Repairing carpets is a fast dying art and there are very few professional craftsmen who will undertake such a job as re-tufting a carpet. So if you have good carpets, you are even more duty bound to repair them yourself—or buy new ones.

Re-tufting

Tufts clawed out by pets, burned out by cigarettes or torn out by carelessly used knee kickers when laying are among the most common forms of surface damage to a carpet.

To make a repair, your first requirement is some matching pile yarn. If the carpet is still in production, you can get this through the retailer from the manufacturers, who will need to know the range name and pattern number—sometimes a small cutting of waste suffices to verify the colours. Most manufacturers are very helpful about supplying matching yarn and often do so free of charge.

If you cannot obtain the correct match, something fairly close is usually available in a knitting wool of a similar gauge. The

Below: *There are various ways of replacing a worn patch of carpet. Here, a latex adhesive is being applied to a new piece of tufted carpet*

only equipment needed for re-tufting is a medium-sized pair of very sharp scissors and a half-round needle with a diameter of about 50mm.

Start by isolating the damaged tufts and snip them off level with the backing, taking care not to cut the backing in the process.

Now thread the needle with about 450mm of the yarn and simply sew it from the surface, in and out of the weft backing. This forms a simple U-shaped tuft of the same proportions as the previous one, except that it should be cut off about 25mm above the surrounding unworn pile.

Continue in this way until the whole patch is filled in. With a patterned carpet, different coloured yarns should be used and the tufts correctly located in accordance with the design. Having sewn in all the tufts, smooth them out in the direction of

1 *Cut a square section from a piece of spare carpet as a replacement piece, making sure that the pile direction is the same*

2 *Place the section squarely over the damaged area and cut round the template piece with the knife blade angled inwards*

3 *When the damaged piece has been removed, apply a latex-based adhesive liberally along each of the edges of the replacement piece*

4 *Stick a piece of one-sided self-adhesive carpet tape under each side of the square and press the carpet down to make the tape stick*

5 *Position the replacement piece down at one end, making sure that the pile runs in the right direction, and push it into place at the seams*

6 *To get the foam rubber seams to stick firmly together push down into the join with the back of the blade of a handyman's knife*

the pile and snip them off level with the rest of the pile.

Complete repairs

If damage to a carpet extends below the level of the pile into the backing structure, a new piece of carpet has to be set in. For this you need a sharp trimming knife with a few heavy-duty blades, a thin, metal straight-edge and a curved needle. The method of repair varies for each type of carpet.

Axminsters and Wiltons: Mark out the extremities of the damage with pins, pushing them right through the backing. With the carpet folded over, the pins enable you to locate the area of damage from the reverse side.

Use your handyman's knife to cut out the damaged portion in a square or rectangular shape, following the line of the weave. The cut must be deep enough to cut and separate the backing without damaging the overhanging pile, which will be needed later to cover the join.

Next place the damaged cut-out on the replacement piece, with the pattern matching, and mark the position with pins pushed right through. Turn it over and cut out the piece required for the repair, following the weave and cutting only just through the backing as before.

Before securing the new piece of carpet in position, seal all raw edges with a proprietary latex compound and allow this to dry. Then place the new piece of carpet into the prepared cut-out, making sure it is the right way round, with the pattern matching and pile direction corresponding.

The edges must be sewn firmly together on the backing section with an over and over stitch using the curved needle and a stout thread. Most carpet suppliers sell carpet thread specially for this purpose.

Finally, apply a 35mm-wide coat of latex compound to the back of the seam and cover this with a fabric tape. Apply gentle pressure on the area and allow it to dry.

Tufted carpets with non-foam backing: The repair method for these is similar to that for Axminsters and Wiltons except that there is no weave structure to follow when cutting out the damaged and replacement sections. Some tufted carpets appear to have a weave structure but this is only a layer of woven material which is stuck on the back and should be disregarded.

The best way to repair this type of carpet is to cut a generous amount of replacement piece into a square or rectangle and place it directly over the worn section. This becomes a template around which you cut into the carpet with the trimming knife angled inwards. Follow figs 7 to 13.

Foam-backed (cushion-backed) carpets: These are just tufted carpets with a foam backing and can be repaired as above—but do not use sewing or fabric tape. Instead, having cut out the replacement piece and placed it in the squared-off damaged area, bond the edges of the foam together with a fine bead of impact adhesive. Then complete the joints with a 50mm-wide self-adhesive carpet tape and allow this to set for about two hours before turning the carpet back into position (see figs 1 to 6).

General maintenance

Regular vacuuming is an essential part of carpet maintenance and is the only effective way to remove damaging grit which becomes embedded in the pile. If you leave this grit for a long time rapid deterioration occurs at the base of the pile.

It is worth having your vacuum cleaner regularly serviced, as it performs a very important job. Upright vacuum cleaners, for instance, need a new drive belt and brush inserts in the beater about every six to 12 months but this you can do yourself.

Carpets fall into two categories according to the type of vacuum which best suits them. Shag-pile carpets are a special case.

Wool carpets: Cylinder-type vacuum cleaners can be used on this type of carpet as and when required at any time during the carpet's life. However, the upright type of cleaner with revolving beater bar and brushes should not be used on a new wool carpet for about six months. Prior to this, the fibres in the yarn will not have had a

7 *For a larger area of damage knock nails through the corners of the replacement piece and underlay to hold it in place*

12 *Place the adhesive also on underside edges of the replacement piece and, with the hessian tape in position, join together*

chance to interlock sufficiently and may be pulled out.

Upright vacuum cleaners are easier to use and often more efficient but they are a little harsher on the pile than cylinder types and so should not be used more than once a week during the initial period.

Man-made fibre carpets: These can have an upright vacuum cleaner used on them from the day they are laid but limit this, if possible, to once a week. A cylinder-type vacuum cleaner can be used as often as required without risk of damage.

Shag-pile carpets: This type of carpet requires special care as the pile becomes tangled and flat if it is not regularly combed

8 *Cut round the template in the manner shown in fig. 2. This is made much easier by the nails that are holding the template in place*

13 *Push the seams into place in the same way as in fig. 6, then knock along each join lightly with a hammer to bed the edges to the tape*

out with a special shag rake. You can buy one of these from any good carpet shop and it takes only a few moments to rake an average-size room. Shag-pile carpets are not designed for heavy use, but if they are subject to a lot of wear they should be raked every day. For vacuuming, use a suction-only cleaner or a heavy-duty upright with a high pile adjustment.

Lifting crush marks

Crush marks from heavy furniture can sometimes be removed by gentle brushing with a small, stiff brush but, if this fails, the

9 *For this non foam-backed tufted carpet you need to cut four lengths of hessian carpet tape to stick under each side*

10 *Spread the latex adhesive solution liberally on one side of the hessian carpet tape and let it dry for a few minutes*

11 *In order to obtain a really firm bind, spread more of the latex adhesive along the underside edges of the carpet*

A. *To soak up stains, blot the spill two or three times using clean tissues under a heavy book*

B. *To lift crushed pile iron lightly over a damp piece of cotton cloth, then comb the pile in the same direction as the rest*

controlled application of steam can work wonders.

First vacuum the area to make sure it is quite clean, then cover the crush mark with a wet, white cotton cloth. Set a steam iron to suit the material of the carpet and hold it over the cloth so that it just touches (fig. B). The resulting steam will then start to lift the pile—an action which you can assist by gently brushing against the pile after each application.

Steam only for a few minutes at a time, checking the effect as you go—over-steaming causes the yarn to untwist. Never allow the iron to be in direct contact with the pile and re-wet the cloth at frequent intervals. Leave the pile sloping in the right direction and allow it to dry. After this treatment the carpet will soon look as good as new again.

★ WATCH POINT ★

High tufts and loose ends are sometimes present in new carpets, but are more likely to be caused by snagging with a sharp object. Never pull out a loose end or tuft standing above the level of the pile: this only causes more damage. Instead, simply snip them off level with the other tufts using a pair of sharp scissors.

Carpet cleaning

Before embarking on cleaning a whole carpet, clear the room of furniture and vacuum away all loose dirt and grit. Two methods of cleaning are easily possible at home: shampooing which can either be done by hand or special machine, and hot water extraction (steam cleaning).

Though simple, shampooing is not particularly satisfactory as it tends to leave a sticky residue in the pile which is very difficult to remove. The residue in turn attracts more dirt and the carpet soon becomes dirty again.

By comparison, the hot water extraction

method leaves no residue at all. The system works by forcing a jet of partly vaporized hot water into the pile of the carpet via a hand-held nozzle. This will loosen and break down the particles of dirt, which are then drawn out of the pile by a powerful vacuum which is in another section of the same nozzle.

Hot water extraction machines can be hired by the day from carpet shops. They are fairly simple to use, though overwetting of the carpet must be avoided as it causes shrinkage.

Treatment for spillages

Never start by rubbing the affected area, as this only drives the stain further into the carpet. Deal with the spillage immediately and gently—scoop up as much as possible with a spoon and then mop with white tissues.

★ WATCH POINT ★

With fairly fluid stains, remarkable results can be obtained by placing a thick wad of tissues over the affected area, weighted down with, say, a heavy book. During a period of 20 minutes or so, natural capillary action draws much of the stain into the tissues. For heavy stains, change the wad of tissues several times. When you are dealing with old or stubborn stains, which are likely to cause problems, it is probably wisest to call in professional assistance.

Particularly important points to remember when attempting to remove the various types of carpet stains are:
● Always work with a clean, white cotton rag or white tissues
● Gently dab or wipe the stain, working inwards
● Never use excessive pressure as this only rubs the stain further in
● Change the tissue or rag as soon as it becomes soiled
● Avoid overwetting and keep stain removers out of the backing
● Leave the pile sloping in the right direction
● Allow carpets to dry before walking on them
● Always test stain removal treatments on a spare piece of carpet.

Dealing with stains

STAIN	TREATMENT
Beer	A squirt from the soda syphon; sponge, rinse and blot dry
Blood	A squirt from the soda syphon; sponge, rinse with cold water and blot dry
Candle wax	Scrape off as much as possible. Melt and absorb the remainder by covering with blotting paper and applying the toe of a warm iron. Do not let the iron come into direct contact with the carpet or use this method with polypropylene or nylon carpets. Dab with methylated spirit to remove any remaining colour
Chewing gum	Treat with any proprietary chewing gum remover or dry cleaning fluid
Coffee	As for beer, but remove final traces with a dry cleaning solvent
Egg	Remove with salt water and blotting paper
Ice cream	Mild carpet shampoo solution; sponge, rinse with warm water and blot dry. Finish with a dry cleaning solvent
Ink	A squirt from the soda syphon; sponge, rinse with warm water and blot dry. Finish with dry cleaning fluid if mark persists
Lipstick	Gently wipe away with paint remover, rinse with warm water and blot dry

STAIN	TREATMENT
Milk	A squirt from the soda syphon; sponge, rinse and blot dry. Follow with mild carpet shampoo solution; sponge, rinse and blot dry. Finish with dry cleaning fluid
Soft drinks	Sponge with mild carpet shampoo solution; rinse with warm water and blot dry
Soot	Vacuum up as much as possible and treat with dry cleaning fluid
Tar	Gently scrape up the deposit. Soften with a solution of 50 per cent glycerine and 50 per cent water. Leave for up to an hour, gently wipe, rinse and blot dry. Obstinate marks can sometimes respond to treatment with dry cleaning fluid or eucalyptus oil
Tea	A squirt from the soda syphon; sponge, rinse and blot dry. Finish with peroxide, 250ml to 250ml water
Urine	A squirt from the soda syphon; sponge and rinse. Sponge with mild carpet shampoo solution, rinse and blot. Then rinse several times using cold water with a few drops of antiseptic added. Blot dry
Wine	Remove with glycerine or peroxide diluted in an equal proportion of water

MENDING CHINA

Few of us go for very long without cracking or breaking a piece of china, and if the object in question is a favourite ornament, it makes sense to repair it. There's more to mending china than simply sticking the bits back together, but if you use the right materials and techniques, you can restore a treasure surprisingly well.

When to repair

Unless a piece of crockery is obviously valuable you should think twice before attempting to repair it. Mending china is painstaking work and repairs can never be 100 per cent perfect, so it's usually easier to give the broken object up for lost. This is particularly sound advice if you have broken one piece from a set and there is a chance that you'll be able to replace it—at an end-of-year remnants sale, for example. China which you serve food from should never be repaired; the cracks, however small, will harbour a build-up of germs.

There are two main types of china—pottery and porcelain. Pottery is clay which has been fired at relatively low temperatures and then had a harder, often pigmented, glaze baked on to it. When it breaks, the glaze usually flakes and chips, and the softer clay underneath may crumble, making repairs difficult.

Porcelain is fired at higher temperatures so that it becomes vitrified—like glass—and consequently does not have a separate glaze. When it breaks it does so cleanly, and

Above: *A repair worth tackling. Porcelain breaks cleanly, so refitting the handle should present no problems*

although it may chip, the chances of making a successful repair are much higher than happens to be the case with porcelain.

Removing dirt and stains

Removing stains is not only a repair job in its own right—it is essential to clean any piece of china before mending it. Adhesive will not form a bond with dirt and grease—the pieces may stay together for a while, but one knock and they'll fall apart.

First remove any surface grease and dirt by scrubbing the piece with a toothbrush or

nailbrush in warm, soapy water—this will show up any underlying stains (fig. 1).

For stubborn surface marks and light scaling, a non-metallic kitchen scourer is a useful aid but use it carefully as the modern types are very hard and may scratch delicate or painted finishes.

For really stubborn stains, and on all china with painted or gilded decoration, make up a solution of one part 100 vol. hydrogen peroxide and three parts water with a few drops of ammonia. You can buy hydrogen peroxide from your local chemist, but take care when using it as it's a strong bleach. If the piece is pottery, soak the area around the stain in water to stop it spreading.

Dab the solution on the stain with cotton wool and leave the swab in place. Repeat with a fresh swab every two to three hours until the stain disappears. If the stains are caused by hardwater scale, dab on some vinegar or lemon juice and then rub them off with a non-metallic kitchen scourer.

Dry the piece carefully after cleaning, using a silk or lint cloth that won't deposit fluff on the surface. Use a pipe cleaner or a piece of wire wrapped in lint for spouts and other awkward places.

If you're removing dirt and stains from broken pieces, you've probably got little to lose by doing the job yourself. But if you find some old china which you think might be valuable, take it for a valuation before attempting to clean it. Many of today's abrasive cleaners are simply too strong for works of art and could ruin them.

1 *Clean all broken china before repairing it. Warm, soapy water will remove surface dirt. Use a toothbrush*

2 *Soak plain pottery and porcelain in an 8:1 bleach solution to remove stains. Dry pottery in an oven afterwards*

3 *Remove stubborn stains by applying a hydrogen peroxide/water/ammonia solution with cotton wool*

4 *To remove stains around spouts and intricate handles, use a pipe cleaner or lint wrapped around wire*

5 *Gummed tape and ordinary plastic film will pull both parts of the repair fully together*

6 *Use a hair dryer to warm the plastic film and make it shrink to the size of the repair*

7 *Make your own form of clamping jig utilizing some battens and some strong elastic bands*

8 *Sometimes one elastic band will provide all the support that is needed to keep the repair together*

Holding and clamping

Adhesive only gives a strong bond if applied under pressure—this goes for china as much as for any other material. Always work out how to apply the pressure before actually making the repair. You'll probably need to experiment, but time spent at this stage is well worth it.

Often the weight of an object or of a broken piece is enough to apply sufficient pressure if it is left to set in the right position. The rule in this case is find the position and then devise a successful way of holding the object in place.

Plates can be held on edge in a slightly opened drawer. A refinement of this technique is to place the object in a box of foam chippings or sand, though if you use sand take extra care that no excess adhesive seeps out of the repair or else grit may contaminate the join.

If you can get it, heat-shrinkable plastic film can be used in the same way: simply wrap the film around the object then heat it with a hair dryer to shrink it and draw the repair together. Take care, though, not to let excess adhesive come into contact with the film. (Heat-shrinkable film is available as the major part of some simple secondary glazing systems.)

Elastic bands, the broader the better, are very useful for holding on things like handles and knobs. Have several sizes of band handy: an overstretched band is likely to collapse the piece, whereas a slack band won't consolidate the join. On certain jobs —especially plates and shallow bowls—you may find it useful to place the object on a board and mark its outline with tacks. You can then use elastic bands stretched between the tacks to hold it in position.

Other useful clamping objects include clothes pegs, bulldog clips, jubilee clips, paper clips and blue sticking putty. But be warned: some of these have a strong clamping action, so take special care not to shift the repair out of alignment.

Gluing techniques

When gluing china, there are several general rules to follow:

★ WATCH POINT ★

Check that the pieces are in perfect alignment by running a piece of stiff plastic—such as a credit card—lightly across them and seeing if it catches. For very small faults, a finger nail is a more sensitive alternative.

● Repair the object as soon as possible after it has been broken. If you can't mend it immediately, gather up all the bits—however small they are—and put them in an envelope.
● Make sure that all the pieces are scrupulously clean—and dry—before gluing.
● Plan the repair. Always stick small pieces to larger ones, and if you have a lot of fragments glue them together into one large assembly and let the adhesive set hard before sticking it in place. If you are in any doubt of the fit, test-fit the pieces before gluing.
● With adhesives, the thinner the film and the more even the coverage, the stronger the repair will be. If you apply so much that it squeezes out when you bring the pieces together, the chances are you've probably used too much.
● Always have some solvent handy to wipe away excess adhesive immediately. Methylated spirit or acetone (available from chemists) can be used with epoxies; only acetone will dissolve 'super' glues.

With most china adhesives, you glue one edge only (but check with the manufacturer's instructions). Apply the glue with a metal object—a knitting needle, knife blade, nail file—as thinly and as evenly as possible. Bring the broken pieces together with light, even pressure: press too hard and you may crumble the edges or the glaze.

Clean away any excess glue straight away, using a cotton bud dipped in the appropriate solvent. Don't touch the joint with your finger.

Position or clamp the repair immediately, taking care not to misalign it. Always follow the manufacturer's recommended drying time for the glue.

Colour matching: If you don't propose to do any more work on the piece after gluing, it's worth colouring the glue to hide the cracks.

The best white pigment is titanium dioxide, available as a powder or as brilliant white enamel from hardware stores. Add it to the glue after you have mixed the resin and hardener together. For colour tinting, use modeller's enamel paint in the same way.

Filling cracks and holes

These are best filled with proprietary epoxy filler, which can either be tinted when you mix it or painted over afterwards. White tinting is achieved by rolling the filler in

9 *Press the filler firmly into the crack—a card helps to establish the necessary profile*

10 *When completely dry, sand the filler lightly with garnet paper or emery cloth until smooth*

11 *If you haven't tinted the filler you've used, paint over it to blend in with the existing colour*

12 *Varnish all over the finished repair to achieve a perfect and even-looking finish*

titanium dioxide powder after mixing, but few chinas are pure white—they invariably contain minute traces of red, blue, yellow or all three. You can also tint adhesive.

To obtain a perfect match, mix up a small quantity of filler with dashes of the appropriately coloured enamel and try it for match on an unobtrusive area of the object; this process takes time, but it's worth it. When you've achieved a perfect match, mix the main batch and press it into the crack with a spatula—a sliver of old credit card or a kitchen knife will do—leaving it slightly proud of the surface. When dry, sand the filler down lightly with garnet paper or emery cloth.

For a really good finish, coat the repair with clear varnish or, better still, a proprietary glazing compound available from DIY centres. These come in one or two-part packs; once mixed and applied with an artist's paintbrush, they can be baked hard in the oven to simulate the china's original glaze.

Painted areas: These are best touched in after filling. Having obtained a good colour match with your enamel, mix in a little glazing compound before you apply the paint. Bake in the oven afterwards—following the manufacturer's instructions—to harden the repair.

Filling holes: Again, this can be done with epoxy filler. Start by taping a piece of plastic card or stiff polythene across the most obtrusive side of the hole, making sure that it follows the surrounding profile (fig. 9).

Mix up the filler and gently press it in from the other side.

When dry, remove the plastic former and fill any pin-prick holes left in the repair. Finish off by sanding down the repair on both sides before retouching in the usual way (fig. 12).

The methods just outlined can be used to make repairs to all broken pieces of commonplace and fine china but you may be lucky enough to have a piece that is collectable. In this case, consider having it restored professionally as this will maximize the value and may improve the appearance too.

What glue to use

The best adhesives for china repairs are the

Above: *Hold glued plates on their edge in a slightly open drawer for quite a while*

two-part epoxy and acrylic resins, which combine high strength with a long open-time—essential if the work is at all fiddly. Their one drawback is that they set to a rather unsightly brown colour, but this can be overcome by mixing in a little pigment.

There may be times when a faster setting glue is essential, in which case opt for a quick setting epoxy rather than a general household repair glue.

Cyanoacrylate 'super' glues do have their

uses in china repairing, particularly as they are colourless when set. They should be confined, however, to clean breaks in fine porcelain which can be repaired instantly: their lack of filling power makes them unsuitable for the crumbly edges of most pottery.

Fillers nearly always have an important part to play. The best ones are two-part epoxy fillers. You can make a perfectly adequate substitute for epoxy fillers by mixing ordinary epoxy resin adhesive with an inert filler such as Plaster of Paris and a colouring pigment.

Restoring old plates

If you have an old, cracked antique plate it may have already been repaired in the past with Scotch glue, plaster and staple rivets, in which case it's worth taking it apart and restoring it using modern materials.

First, soak the plate in boiling water for a few hours to loosen the plaster around the rivets; you can then ease the latter out with pliers.

The glue on the plate may prove harder to shift; if further soakings don't work, saturate the crack with paint stripper applied from a swab (wear rubber gloves).

When the plate falls apart, thoroughly clean away all the remains of old glue off the edges before attempting to make a new repair.

When you examine the cleaned plate, the two halves may no longer align. This is because the fracture has released the tensions that build up when a piece is fired. Don't worry if this is the case—it is possible to clamp a plate progressively so that it fits together again but you need to work slowly and carefully.

INDEX

Picture credits
The Camden Studio: 29.
Gavin Cochrane: 4–9,
    10–15, 60.
Ray Duns: 25–28, 30–34,
    35–39, 61–62, 64–68.
Nelson Hargreaves: 16–20.
Dave King: 54.
Bill McLaughlin: 59.
Nigel Messett: 46–50.
Roger Payling: 69–71.
Ray Rathbone/Sunday
    Times: 63(b).
Victor Watts: 3.